P9-DMY-999

Authentic
Beauty
GOING DEEPER

Authentic *Beauty*

GOING DEEPER

a study guide
for the set-apart young woman

Leslie Ludy

MULTNOMAH
BOOKS

AUTHENTIC BEAUTY, GOING DEEPER
PUBLISHED BY MULTNOMAH BOOKS
12265 Oracle Boulevard, Suite 200
Colorado Springs, Colorado 80921
A division of Random House Inc.

All Scripture quotations, unless otherwise indicated, are taken from the New American Standard Bible®. © Copyright The Lockman Foundation 1960, 1962, 1963, 1968, 1971, 1972, 1973, 1975, 1977, 1995. Used by permission. (www.Lockman.org). Scripture quotations marked (KJV) are taken from the King James Version. Scripture quotations marked (NKJV) are taken from the New King James Version®. Copyright © 1982 by Thomas Nelson Inc. Used by permission. All rights reserved. Scripture quotations marked (NEB) are taken from the New English Bible. Copyright © 1961, 1970 by the Delegates of the Oxford University Press and the Syndics of the Cambridge University Press. Scripture quotations marked (NIV) are taken from the Holy Bible, New International Version®. NIV®. Copyright © 1973, 1978, 1984 by International Bible Society. Used by permission of Zondervan Publishing House. All rights reserved.

Italics in Scripture quotations indicate the author's added emphasis.

ISBN 978-1-59052-975-1

Copyright © 2007 by Leslie Ludy

Published in association with Loyal Arts Literary Agency, LoyalArts.com.

All rights reserved. No part of this book may be reproduced or transmitted in any form or by any means, electronic or mechanical, including photocopying and recording, or by any information storage and retrieval system, without permission in writing from the publisher.

MULTNOMAH is a trademark of Multnomah Books and is registered in the U.S. Patent and Trademark Office. The colophon is a trademark of Multnomah Books.

Library of Congress Cataloging-in-Publication Data

Printed in the United States of America
2007—First Edition

10 9 8 7 6 5 4 3 2 1

❧ Contents

Contents

PART III: ROMANTIC MYSTIQUE
The Mystery of a Set-Apart Young Woman

PART IV: TENDER REVERENCE
The Passion of a Set-Apart Young Woman

A Word of Thanks

I WOULD LIKE to express my deepest thanks to six very special young women: To Kendra Sensenig, for tirelessly and diligently compiling all the material for this study guide—this project wouldn't have happened without you! And to Ashley Obendorf, Annie Wesche, Brianne Totman, Megan King, and Gabi Dutzmann, thank you for your assistance, suggestions, and valuable contributions—especially for being vulnerable enough to include your own personal stories in this study guide. I am blessed and honored to have you all as my friends. I hope we have many more unforgettable times together sitting around that little coffee table!

Introduction

IN OUR HOUSE, there is a cozy room with four Manhattan-style leather chairs positioned in a circle around a small coffee table. It's our favorite place to go for writing, thinking, daydreaming, and visiting with friends. Grasping oversized mugs of hot chocolate or chai in our hands, we sit across from each other and enjoy glimpses of the majestic Rocky Mountains in the distance. It's a peaceful room, one that invites intimate conversation. Eric and I have spent hours talking in those overstuffed chairs, exploring truth, recalling funny memories, and recounting life's many adventures. We've also shared many wonderful moments with others around that circle of chairs, playing games, telling stories, and laughing, crying, and praying with our friends and family.

But one of my favorite experiences in that cozy room happened last fall, when a group of four young women met there for a time of prayer, encouragement, and exploring the message of *Authentic Beauty* together. They were the first members of the Authentic Girl Ministry Team, four girls who had rearranged their lives in order to move to Colorado and join me in ministering to today's young women.

None of the girls knew one another before moving to Colorado to share a house, a life, and a ministry. They all had different backgrounds, different personalities, different interests, and different dreams and desires. But there was one thing that each one of those young women held at the center of her being: a passion for the set-apart life. Each one longed to build her existence fully and completely around Jesus Christ. And because of that mutual passion, there was an instant, eternal bond that was formed among them. Instead of feeling alone and isolated in their set-apart journeys, they now had the encouragement, support, companionship, and prayers of five other young women on the same path.

The first time I sat across from these four young women in our circle of chairs, I could sense the significance of what was taking place. It was as if a "Fellowship of the Set-Apart" was being formed, a sacred circle of friendship, trust, accountability, and unity in Jesus Christ. As we began discussing the message of *Authentic Beauty*, the girls shared their own stories of how God had called each of them to a set-apart existence. They spoke of their struggles, doubts, fears, and victories along the way. And everyone in the room was uplifted, comforted, and strengthened as each girl spoke. We met together every week, and through those precious times of fellowship, each member was challenged and equipped to pursue Christ even further into His endless frontier. Each of the girls encouraged and motivated the others to remain rooted and strong in the set-apart existence.

Today, when people look at the lives of these four young women, they see something that makes them sit back in wonder. They see radiance, mystique, and selflessness. They see a passion for Jesus Christ that far outweighs any other pursuit or desire. They see "the few" in this generation who have chosen to follow a completely different path than the rest of the culture. They see lilies among thorns.

It is my hope and prayer that as you explore the message of *Authentic Beauty*—whether individually or with a group—you will not feel you are on this journey alone. I invite you to join our Fellowship of the Set-Apart; to hold your mug of hot chocolate and sit across from me and the other girls in those cozy leather chairs; to be encouraged, inspired, challenged, uplifted, and, most of all, equipped to live a set-apart existence for Jesus Christ.

Becoming a set-apart young woman is not an easy path to walk. There will be doubts, loneliness, discouragement, and even ridicule from the world around you. But a life fully yielded to Christ is the only life truly worth living. It is the most fulfilling, adventurous, exciting existence you could ever experience.

As you go through this study, I encourage you to allow God to personalize it to your own situation. Not all the suggestions or ideas may apply to you, but I hope they will serve as catalysts for the unique work God wants to do in your own life. If you find there is a particular question or story that speaks to you, I encourage you to spend the majority of your time there rather than feel a need to get through all the questions in a particular section. The important thing is not to complete this study guide but rather to allow God's Spirit to direct you through this journey in a personal way. To get the most out of this experience, you may find it helpful to have a Bible and a writing journal with you as you read.

Please know that even though I may not know your name, you are in my prayers as you embark upon this journey. I pray that through this study you will draw closer to Christ than ever before and that your life will never be the same again.

A Note for Group Leaders

If you are taking a group through this study guide, here are some things that may be helpful to keep in mind.

Questions are divided into three sections within each chapter. The first two sections—"Opening Up" and "The Next Level"—are designed to facilitate meaningful group discussion. Many of these questions are general, but they get progressively more personal, so be aware that some people in your group may not feel comfortable answering all the questions out loud. I've included a few scripture suggestions that correspond with many of the questions. You can choose to incorporate them or leave them out, depending on the needs and dynamics of your group.

The third section of questions—"For Personal Reflection, Prayer, and Study"—is designed for individual focus and meditation. You could encourage group members to tackle these questions at home each week, or you might want to carve out some time during your meeting for each person to spend some time alone with God going over these questions. It would be helpful for each person to have a Bible, pen, and journal as she works through this section.

The "Overcoming Roadblocks" section at the end of each chapter addresses some of the most common questions that young women ask about living a set-apart life. These sections can be used to facilitate group discussions, or you can encourage group members to read these sections on their own at home each week. Similarly, you may want your group to read the boxed sections of each chapter during the week, or you may want to use one or two of the pieces as a springboard for further discussion.

Just as this book needs to be personalized for an individual, it will be most effective if you personalize it to the needs of your group. You will probably find that the dynamics of your group change as you progress through the book, so feel free to adjust how you use the questions and other sections throughout the course of the study.

For additional resources on living the set-apart life or to find out more about our ministry for today's young women, I would encourage you to visit our Web site, www.authenticgirl.com.

the first
step

understanding

the

crisis

facing

modern-day

femininity

1

The Erosion of a
Feminine Dream

$\mathcal{D}$EEP WITHIN the feminine heart lies a God-given longing to be valued, cherished, and found beautiful by a noble, gallant prince. But we live in a world that seeks to destroy that desire. In our desperate attempts to find a fairy tale, most of us have ended up with only broken hearts and shattered dreams.

OPENING UP

1. Would you say that femininity is in crisis in our culture? Why or why not? How do you think most young women today view femininity?

2. Why do you think so many young women today are giving up on the dream of finding beautiful, lasting love?

3. Would you say that manhood is in crisis in our culture? Why or why not? How do you think most guys today view masculinity?

4. Do you feel that our society mocks the idea of fairy-tale romance? If so, in what specific ways have you seen this?

The LORD is near to the brokenhearted
And saves those who are crushed in spirit. (Psalm 34:18)

As you embark upon this study, let me encourage you: no matter how many times you have been hurt, rejected, violated, or disappointed, there is One who loves you more than you could ever comprehend. Whatever your background or present circumstances, I pray that He would soften and prepare your heart to experience His amazing love, restoration, and hope like never before.

THE NEXT LEVEL

1. In what ways is the story in chapter 1 similar to or different from your own life?

2. Do you have a desire for a knight in shining armor who will sweep you off your feet? Have you ever tried to fulfill that desire through a relationship with a guy? What was the result?

3. In what ways does the influence of the world (guys, school, pop culture, etc.) affect your perspective on your own femininity? How has it caused you to lower your standards or be tempted to lower your standards?

Shattered Dreams

(EXCERPT FROM *WHEN DREAMS COME TRUE*)

I will never forget the night we broke up. I remember throwing myself across my bed, my body racked with heartbroken sobs. I felt like something inside had died. It was like someone had taken my delicate heart and fragile emotions, ripped them out, and shattered them all over the ground into a million pieces. My security was gone. I didn't know who I was anymore. I didn't even want to live.

I knew I had lost something precious in the process of my relationship with Brandon. I had given away the deepest part of me to someone who no longer appreciated it, no longer wanted it.

I longed for the pain to go away. I became like an addict, compromising myself physically and emotionally with guys I barely knew, only to wake up the next day feeling sick with remorse but powerless to stop myself.

Looking back, it all runs together like a nightmarish dream.

And amazingly, through it all, there was a God watching me fall, watching me break His heart, and loving me still. He was waiting on the other side of my shattered dreams with some dreams of His own.[1]

4. How does the influence of the world affect your dream of lasting, beautiful romance? Have you given away your heart or body as a result? What were the main influences in your life that contributed to that decision?

FOR PERSONAL REFLECTION, PRAYER, AND STUDY

1. Ask God to reveal to you any harmful messages, thoughts, and habits that have crept into your life as a result of living in this culture.

2. Ask God to show you the ways you might currently be giving away your heart, emotions, mind, body, and innocence in order to find fulfillment. Write down what you feel He is speaking to your heart.

3. Write down any areas of your life that you are confused about (for example, guys, a relationship, purity). Ask God to reveal His life-changing truth to you about each of these areas as you embark upon this study.

2

The Reviving of the Feminine Heart

*J*ESUS CHRIST IS our true Prince: the One we have been longing for, searching for, and dreaming of since childhood. The One who will love us the way no one else can love us. The One who will cherish us forever. The One who will transform us from hopeless girls in rags into beautiful, confident, radiant princesses.

OPENING UP

1. Why do you think so many young women seek fulfillment through one short-term relationship after another? Do they find what they are looking for through this pattern? Why or why not?

   Because they're looking for the man who will fullfill their dream man. What they want. Doesn't usually work because a lot of the time they're not trusting God + having faith + hope.

2. Why is it so easy for us as young women to define our identities by the way guys treat us? What are some of the biggest dangers in doing this?

   Because we're with them so often + if we want to keep them, sometimes that's what it takes.

3. Do you think it is difficult for most young women to see Christ as their true Prince? Why or why not?

   Yes because of the environment we live in today.

THE NEXT LEVEL

1. Who is Jesus Christ to you? a flimsy flannel-board character? a distant
   being in heaven? the One who saved you from your sins? Describe your
   current relationship with Christ. Be as honest as possible.

   *I have a strong relationship with Christ. He is my Knight
   & shining armor who died on the cross with. for me we actually
   have a relationship, a friendship.*

2. What kind of relationship do you want to have with Jesus Christ? Do you
   find it easy or difficult to believe He desires a beautiful, intimate, daily
   romance with you? Why?

   *I want a loving relationship with Christ.
   I find it easy to believe this because I know
   I wouldn't be able to go each day without
   him. I know when I'm upset he comforts me.*

3. Have there been times in your life when you experienced deep, daily intimacy with Christ? If so, what were some of the specific things you experienced and learned in your relationship with Him?

   *when I listen to music & when I go camping
   in N.H. with the teens from my church.*

FOR PERSONAL REFLECTION, PRAYER, AND STUDY

1. Do you doubt Christ's passionate love and intense desire for you? Read through these verses that testify to His love: **Jeremiah 29:11; Jeremiah 31:3; Zephaniah 3:17; John 3:16;** and **1 John 3:1.** Remember, these words were written by Him to you. What is He speaking to your heart through these verses?

   I do not doubt anything about God.
   God is telling me that He is in control,
   has everything in control and that there's
   no reason to worry. He has promises of love
   to us. Reading these made me feel special
   in a way. It's reasurring.

2. Jesus didn't live His life the way anyone else did. He stood out like a neon billboard on a lonely desert highway. Prayerfully look at your life. Is there any part of your world (friendships, relationships, surroundings) that does not accept Jesus and the lifestyle He calls you to?

Return, return, O Shulamite;
Return, return… (Song of Solomon 6:13, NKJV)

Does this call not demonstrate His strong desire after us, His condescending love for us? It seems so amazing to me that Christ should want our fellowship, but He does—He cannot be happy without us…. I dared not have said this if the Holy Spirit had not declared it, but it is true! Jesus must have us or He is a Bridegroom without a bride…. Oh, how He loves us! How He longs for communion with us! Shall He stand and cry, "Return, return," and will we not come to Him at once?

Hear Him, again, but in another way. He knocks at our door, and He cries, "Open to Me, My sister, My love, My dove, My undefiled, for My head is filled with dew and My locks with the drops of the night." [Song of Solomon 5:2] Will we not admit Him? If He seeks our company and, therefore, calls us to return, our spirit [breaks free from] the bonds that hold [us] on the right and on the left. [We cry,] "Let me go! I must be with my Lord. His voice compels me. My soul would leap out of my body rather than not come to Him who cries, "Return, return, return, return."

CHARLES SPURGEON[2]

3. Are there things in your life that you are unwilling to give up in order to find passionate intimacy with Christ? Ask Him to soften your heart and make you ready and willing to become fully His. Read **John 12:24–26** and write down what He is speaking to your heart.

4. Jesus Christ is longing for you. He is standing outside your dungeon window, patiently waiting for you to hear His gentle voice and allow Him to rescue you, redeem you, and transform your entire existence. He is inviting you to embark upon the most breathtaking, beautiful, passionate, romantic adventure of all time—an eternal love story with your heavenly Prince. Are you ready to respond? If so, write a letter to your Prince. It can be one sentence or several pages. In your own words, express what is taking place in your heart. What do you want to tell Christ as you offer Him your life?

Overcoming Roadblocks

Is it too late?

When contemplating an intimate romance with Jesus Christ, it's easy to think, *This is too good to be true. I've made too many mistakes. I am beyond the point of experiencing a beautiful love story with Him.*

If that is what you are feeling, go to Him with your doubts. Ask Him to show you His infinite love and desire for you. Be encouraged by the following account in Scripture about a woman who was completely undeserving of Christ's love and forgiveness. Observe the way Christ responded to her. This is the way He responds to each of us when we come to Him in true repentance:

Let us be glad and rejoice and give Him glory, for the marriage of the Lamb has come, and His wife has made herself ready. (Revelation 19:7, NKJV)

And behold, a woman in the city who was a sinner, when she knew that Jesus sat at the table in the Pharisee's house, brought an alabaster flask of fragrant oil, and stood at His feet behind Him weeping; and she began to wash His feet with her tears, and wiped them with the hair of her head; and she kissed His feet and anointed them with the fragrant oil.

Now when the Pharisee who had invited Him saw this, he spoke to himself, saying, "This Man, if He were a prophet, would know who and what manner of woman this is who is touching Him, for she is a sinner."

And Jesus answered and said to him, "Simon, I have something to say to you." So he said, "Teacher, say it."

"There was a certain creditor who had two debtors. One owed five hundred denarii, and the other fifty. And when they had nothing with which to repay, he freely forgave them both. Tell Me, therefore, which of them will love him more?"

Simon answered and said, "I suppose the one whom he forgave more." And He said to him, "You have rightly judged."

Then He turned to the woman and said to Simon, "Do you see this woman? I entered your house; you gave Me no water for My feet, but she has washed My feet with her tears and wiped them with the hair of her head. You gave Me no kiss, but this woman has not ceased to kiss My feet since the time I came in. You did not anoint My head with oil, but this woman has anointed My feet with fragrant oil. Therefore I say to you, her sins, which are many, are forgiven, for she loved much. But to whom little is forgiven, the same loves little."

Then He said to her, "Your sins are forgiven.... Your faith has saved you. Go in peace." (Luke 7:37–48, 50, NKJV)

Simon the Pharisee didn't feel he needed a Savior. He treated Christ as a casual buddy, hoping to glean some interesting insight or personal benefit from being around Him. That's the way many of us approach Christ today. But that's not true repentance.

The sinful woman knew that Jesus Christ was her only hope. She had come face to face with the ugliness and horror of her sin and defilement. She had accepted her utter unworthiness. And because of this, she could truly receive the mercy and forgiveness of her Lord. She threw herself at His feet in unreserved devotion and gratitude. That is true repentance.

Don't let feelings of unworthiness hold you back. Rather, let your shame and sorrow cause you to fall at His feet. It is only when we *embrace* our own unworthiness that we understand true repentance. When we know how great our debt is, we understand the gravity and wonder of what Christ has done for us. When we are forgiven much, we love Him with unreserved devotion and gratitude.

What about an earthly romance?

We often believe that if we devote our entire lives to Christ, we will miss out on earthly romance. If each of us is passionately pursuing a love story with Jesus Christ instead of desperately searching for the right guy, will we miss our chance for an earthly love story?

The truth is that we will never be able to experience a lasting, God-written earthly love story unless Jesus Christ becomes the first love of our lives and the source of our fulfillment. My romance with Eric is merely an outflow of a much more important romance—my relationship with my true Prince, Jesus Christ. If I look to Eric to meet my needs for joy, security, peace, and emotional fulfillment, I will only be disappointed. Jesus Christ, not an earthly lover, is the only One who can truly

The king's daughter is all glorious within:
Her clothing is of wrought gold.
She shall be brought unto the king in raiment
of needlework:
The virgins her companions that follow her
shall be brought unto thee.
With gladness and rejoicing shall they be brought:
They shall enter into the king's palace.
(Psalm 45:13–15, KJV)

meet the deepest desires of my heart. God is very interested in your earthly romance. In fact, He cares more about that area of your life than even you do! If His plan for you is marriage, you can trust that He will write an amazing, beautiful earthly love story for you if you leave the pen in His hands. But the first step in any God-written love story is for both individuals to be fully surrendered to Jesus Christ as the Lord and Lover of their souls.

lily among *thorns*

the essence

of a set-apart

young woman

Like a lily among the thorns,
so is my darling among the maidens.

SONG OF SOLOMON 2:2

3

Lily White

Beginning the Set-Apart Life

*T*RUE PURITY IS more than simply saving sex until marriage. True purity is complete set-apartness for our heavenly Prince, not just in the area of relationships and sexuality, but in every aspect of our existence.

OPENING UP

1. How does the world around you view feminine purity? Is innocence scoffed at or applauded?

   Innocence can be both in a way... depending on the view. The world views purity as something almost unknown and... weird?

2. In what ways has the attitude that "guys will be guys" lowered your hopes and expectations about men?

   It's sad + depressing. Brings my hopes down a little but there really is no worry/need to because God has everything under control. It's making my faith stronger.

3. In **Matthew 23:25–26**, Jesus says: "Woe to you, scribes and Pharisees, hypocrites! For you cleanse the outside of the cup and dish, but inside they are full of extortion and self-indulgence. Blind Pharisee, first cleanse

the inside of the cup and dish, that the outside of them may be clean also" (NKJV). What has been your definition of *purity* up until now? According to Christ, where does true purity flow from?

Purity is staying clean for your special someone that God has in store for you. Trusting & pleasing the Lord.

Purity flows from your heart & mind.

Purity, I fear, has gotten mixed up in people's minds with "Puritanism," which, in the popular imagination, is a dour, brittle revolt against all the pleasures of the flesh. The concept of purity does not deny life. Rather, it refers back to the very Giver of Life Himself. Purity means freedom from contamination, from anything that would spoil the taste or the pleasure, reduce the power, or in any way adulterate what the thing was meant to be. It means cleanness, clearness—no additives, nothing artificial—in other words, "all natural," in the sense in which the Original Designer designed it to be.

ELISABETH ELLIOT[3]

THE NEXT LEVEL

1. In what ways does the culture around you pressure or influence you to lower your standards in the area of purity?

   The way people act + talk. Also movies + shows act like it's perfectly fine to have sex + that it's weird if you dont... A lot of the time, people want to be just like actors/actresses.

2. What is Christ's standard for the way guys should act and think toward women? Do your words and actions suggest that you have accepted the debased attitude of many modern men, or are you helping them rise to a higher standard? *Scripture suggestions:* **Proverbs 6:25–29; Matthew 5:28; Titus 2:11–12.**

3. What does it mean to give God the throne of your life? If we have been "crucified with Christ" how should that reality look in our lives? *Scripture suggestions:* **Matthew 16:24; Galatians 2:20.**

4. We can easily think we know God, because we know all the Sunday-school answers or have scriptures memorized. But to have a relationship with our Prince, we must seek to know Him intimately, not just know *about* Him. Describe the kind of relationship that Christ wants to have with you. *Scripture suggestions:* **Psalm 84:10; John 15:5–11.**

Better a thousand
times effective
peculiarity
than ineffective
ordinariness.

D. M. THORNTON[4]

FOR PERSONAL REFLECTION, PRAYER, AND STUDY

1. Take a moment to examine your life. Do you feel you are living in true purity? Read **Philippians 4:8; 1 Thessalonians 4:7–8; and 2 Timothy 2:22.** Allow God to convict you where conviction is needed and write down what He is speaking to your heart.

2. Many of us come up with excuses for rejecting God's call to live set-apart lives. On page 46 of *Authentic Beauty,* I summarize some of the most common excuses into three categories: Mud Puddle Girls, Comfort Club Ladies, and Lazy Susans. Read the following definitions, and allow God to show you if and how you have bought into the attitudes below. Then read the corresponding scriptures, and ask God to cleanse you from these mind-sets.

Mud Puddle Girls

Believing the lie that it is too late for you to be forgiven and redeemed.

Read **John 8:1–11** and **Romans 10:11,** and write down what God is speaking to your heart.

Comfort Club Ladies

Believing the lie that you're doing pretty well on your own.

Read **Romans 3:9–12** and **Revelation 3:17**, and write down what God is speaking to your heart.

BECOMING A LILY AMONG THORNS

A life fully transformed by Christ, completely other than this world, is the life that ravishes His heart. I love Amy Carmichael's definition of the set-apart life: "being dead to the world and its applause, to all the customs, fashions and laws of those who hate the humbling Cross."[5] In other words, caring not at all what the world expects or thinks of you, but caring only what Christ expects and thinks…living for the applause of only One.

Lazy Susans
Believing the lie that set-apartness shouldn't be radical or uncomfortable.

Read **John 15:18–19; 2 Timothy 2:21; 3:12;** and **1 Peter 1:15;** and write down what God is speaking to your heart.

3. Too many of us assume that we can intimately know our Prince in the midst of a chaotic, harried life. But, as Henry Blackaby wrote, "We cannot stay where we are and go with God."[6] Our Prince does not live at the frantic pace of this world. His tender whisper is like a still, small voice that is quickly drowned out in our distracted minds. Prayerfully think through and describe the areas of your life that are distracting you from building intimacy with your Prince.

friends, T.V. sports, school...

4. Evaluate the priority level of each area of your life based on how much time, energy, attention, and focus you give to it. In the left column below, write the priority number you feel each of these areas *should* have in your life. Then in the right column, write the priority number each area currently *is* in your life, being as honest as possible. Remember not to assume that something is a top priority because you want it to be. (Use a scale of 1 to 10, with 10 being your highest priority.)

If something in your life is currently ranked above Jesus Christ, ask yourself why. Should you be doing something to change this? (Chapter 4 will talk more about this.) Begin prayerfully considering this question, and write down any thoughts you have.

SHOULD BE	CATEGORIES	CURRENTLY IS	
5	Activities/Hobbies	5 6	4
8	Church	3 8	8
6	Entertainment/Fun		5
9	Family	6 9	9
7	Friends	A A	7
1	Future plans		1
10	Relationship with Christ	10	10
2	Romantic relationships		3
3	School	6 3	5
1	Shopping/Beauty	8	6
4	Work		2

35

5. Jesus's death on the cross was the ultimate romantic gesture of the most pure and perfect love imaginable. Imagine Christ down on one knee, showing you His bloody, nail-scarred palms, saying, *"I did this for you so that I could set you free from sin and death, transform you from a beggar into a royal princess, and make you My own for all eternity. I did this so that My life could invade your being and consume every aspect of your existence. Every moment you are awake, I desire to reveal more of Myself to you. Come away from sin, selfishness, and worldly pursuits. Come away to My beautiful land. Let My life sustain you through richer or poorer, through sickness and health, through all of life's ups and downs. The most glorious romance of all time awaits you. All you have to do is take My hand and say YES!"* In as many or as few words as you desire, write down your heart's response to Christ's words.

Lord, I will take your hand + lay my life
for you. I love you with all my heart. What is
mine is yours + Lord, let me follow your path.
Be my leader. My life is in your hands.
Let your will be done through whatever happens.
Love you & Thanks.... ♥ mwah :)

OVERCOMING ROADBLOCKS

Are there any set-apart guys?

It can be extremely difficult to make the choice to live in true purity for Christ when so many modern men seem to scoff at set-apartness. Most guys seem far more attracted to loose, aggressive, worldly girls than to set-apart princesses of purity. Many of us have the fear that choosing set-apart lives will cause us to live the rest of our days as lonely hermits in the woods, because we can't find guys with godly standards. If you can relate to this concern, let me encourage you in two ways.

First, when making a decision to follow Christ, we must be willing to lay *everything* down at His feet, including our desires for marriage and family. He may choose to fulfill those desires in His own time and way. But our love and devotion for Him must be so complete that even if we never see those dreams realized, we are still willing to offer Him our lives and go wherever He leads us. Read **Luke 9:23**, and ask God to make your heart ready to deny yourself in order to follow Him.

Second, let me assure you that the more that Eric and I travel this world, the more we are meeting amazing, godly, set-apart young men who are praying and waiting for Christ-built princesses of purity. We'll talk more about those kind of guys later in this study. But for now, let your heart be uplifted in knowing that set-apart guys *do* exist—even if you don't see them in your life right now.

He is looking through the windows,
He is peering through the lattice.
My beloved responded and said to me,
"Arise, my darling, my beautiful one,
And come along." (Song of Solomon 2:9–10)

Life Meaning: Our Prince longs for unhindered intimacy with us. But first, we must "arise." We must leave our comfortable lives of apathy and go with Him; our old lives must be left behind. He has given us a new beginning in Him.

Is the standard too high?

As you prepare to embark upon your set-apart journey with Christ, the Enemy may assault you with doubts such as, *This is a little too extreme, don't you think? As long as you are living better than the rest of the girls in this world, you are doing just fine! Why should you have to be so radical in your pursuit of Christ? You don't want to become snobby, legalistic, or holier-than-thou, do you? How will you be able to connect with the world when your life is so different from others?*

But following Christ *is* radical. It is extreme. And it does make others uncomfortable. As long as you are trying to blend Christianity in with your own mediocre existence, you will never experience a passionate romance with your true Prince. Read **Philippians 2:5–8**. Christ loves us with an extreme, sacrificial, even ridiculous love. And He calls us to love Him the very same way. Don't be fooled by the suggestion that following Christ doesn't cost anything. His love for us cost Him everything—even His very life. And our love for Him must cost our very lives in return. Read the story of what He did for you on the cross in **Mark 15**. Be reminded of how radical His love for you is and what it cost Him. And then ask Him to give you the strength to respond to that love with unashamed, radical, sacrificial devotion.

4

The Sacred Sanctuary

Creating the Inward Environment

$\mathcal{I}$N ORDER TO think, act, speak, and live like His princesses every day of our lives, our innermost being must become a set-apart place, a sacred sanctuary worthy of His presence. Our hearts must be transformed into an intimate retreat, unstained by the pollution of the world—where we can discover more and more of Him and allow Him to shape us into His lily-white likeness.

OPENING UP

1. It's easy to compare our lives to the world and assume that God must be happy as long as we are making better moral decisions than most people. What kind of commitment has Christ called us to? How does the true Christian life compare to simply making moral decisions? *Scripture suggestion:* **Romans 12:1–2.**

   Christ has called us to be a witness + to live for God following his commands. In a christian life you do things without caring about what other people think and you do it to please God, not yourself or anyone else. This is unlike making simple, moral decisions.

A warning which needs to be repeated is that "the cares of this world and the deceitfulness of riches," and the lust for other things, will choke out the life of God in us (Matthew 13:22).… Our Lord says to be careful only about one thing—our relationship with Him. But our common sense shouts loudly and says, "That is absurd, I must consider how I am going to live, and I must consider what I am going to eat and drink." Jesus says you must not.… Jesus Christ knows our circumstances better than we do, and He says we must not think about these things to the point where they become the primary concern of our life. Be sure you always put your relationship to God first.

OSWALD CHAMBERS[7]

2. Describe the kind of sacred sanctuary that Christ wants to build within you. *Scripture suggestions:* **Song of Solomon 4:16; 1 Corinthians 6:19.**

   He wants to build a christ-like sanctuary within us.

3. When we learn to focus completely on our Prince, our pursuits and desires change. What does it mean to delight in Him? *Scripture suggestion:* **Psalm 37:4.**

   To delight in him is to praise him and be thankful for all that He's done & created on the Earth. Almost to look up to him and admire.

THE NEXT LEVEL

1. Christ didn't come to earth just to save us from our sins; He came *to give us His very life*. **Romans 5:10** says that "we shall be saved by His life." In

The prophet Elijah…called upon the…Israelites to take the priests of Baal, and sternly cried, "Let not one of them escape." [1 Kings 1:8] He took them all down to the brook Kishon, and slew them there. So must it be with our sins—they are all doomed, not one must be preserved. Our darling sin must die. Spare it not for its much crying. Strike, though it be as dear as an Isaac. Strike, for God struck at sin when it was laid upon His own Son.

With stern unflinching purpose must you condemn to death that sin which was once the idol of your heart. Do you ask how you are to accomplish this? Jesus will be your power. You have grace to overcome sin given you in the covenant of grace; you have strength to win the victory in the crusade against inward lusts, because Christ Jesus has promised to be with you even unto the end…. Let us fly to our God, He is a consuming fire; He will not consume our spirit, but our sins. Let the goodness of God excite us to a sacred jealousy, and to a holy revenge against those iniquities which are hateful in His sight.

CHARLES SPURGEON[8]

other words, when He occupies the center of our hearts and souls, we don't just receive salvation, *we receive His very life.* As we invite the life of Christ to dwell within us and as we continually yield to that life, we will naturally reflect His glorious nature. Think about your own spiritual life. Have you accepted His salvation but stopped short of allowing His life to overtake your existence? Read **Revelation 3:20.** Is He is knocking at the door of your heart? What do you feel He is speaking to you?

I know I have already opened my door. The Lord is controlling my life. I've given it to him.

2. Christ wants to remove our sin from us as far as the east is from the west. Once He has cleansed us, our sin is so far removed from us that it is no longer a part of who we are. It no longer has a hold or claim over our lives. How do you respond to that truth? *Scripture suggestion:* **Psalm 103:11–12.**

It makes me feel relieved and clean. It boosts me to do what pleases God and only that.

BATTLING GUILT AND SHAME

Jordan approached me hesitantly at the end of a Christian leadership conference where Eric and I were speaking. Her haunted blue eyes instantly captured my attention. As we talked, I was struck by her grace and elegance. A tall, athletic blonde, she emanated style and confidence.

Jordan gave me a quick intro to her life: She was active in her church, had loving Christian parents, and was surrounded by wonderful Christian friends. She was gearing up for her first year at a well-known Christian university. On the outside, Jordan's life seemed perfect. But Jordan had a shameful secret. She was involved in an ongoing sexual relationship that no one knew about. "I feel so far away from God right now," she whispered in a tormented voice. "Everyone thinks I am such a great role model for purity. Nobody knows the truth about me."

Jordan's parents often told her, "God has an amazing plan for your life. He is going to bless your future marriage because you are waiting for His best." Their bubbly, well-intentioned words only seemed to mock Jordan's inner misery.

Jordan poured out her desperation to me with a torrent of tears. "I can't seem to stop sinning," she admitted bitterly, "no matter how much I want to. Sometimes I don't even care anymore. I know that it is too late for me to have anything beautiful, so why should I let myself be tortured by all this guilt and shame?"

In today's world, guilt is something to be avoided at all costs, like a dreaded, disfiguring disease. Even in Christian circles, words like *guilt* and *shame* are often taboo. A common sentiment Christian leaders today express is "God doesn't want you to walk around feeling guilty! Just remember that Christ has covered all your sin and let it go!" It's true that God does not want us to wallow in guilt or feelings of worthlessness. But sometimes we become so preoccupied with trying to ignore or cover up our guilt that we fail to recognize that prick on our conscience for what it is: the gentle, loving hand of our Lord, patiently drawing us to Himself.

It is never easy to admit we are headed in the wrong direction. But that is the first, crucial step toward healing, restoration, and discovering the hope and future our Lord has for us.

Jordan felt it was too late for her to discover a beautiful, God-written love story or even to experience a close relationship with Christ again. But nothing could be further from the truth. In fact, her inner turmoil was the first step to an amazing future with Christ. Her guilt was a gentle reminder that her Prince was calling to her—longing for her to abandon her wandering ways and come running back into His loving arms for grace and forgiveness. Just like the shepherd who leaves his entire flock to search for that one lost lamb, our Lord passionately pursues us when we stray from Him. If Jordan's sin had ruined her chance for a hope and a future, why would her Prince be calling her back to Himself?

Repentance means recognizing that we are headed in the wrong direction, then turning around and heading in the right direction. A pang of guilt for unresolved sin in our lives can be a reminder of how much our Prince longs for unhindered intimacy with us. He calls us to acknowledge that we have gone astray and to head in the right direction—toward His eager, healing embrace.

3. When we remove other lovers, we are often getting rid of things in our lives that give us confidence, security, and happiness. Why would God ask us to lay down those things? If God were to ask you, *Am I enough?* how would you respond? *Scripture suggestions:* **Deuteronomy 11:13–15; Proverbs 8:17–21.**

I would say that You are more than enough. I would choose you over anything. You provide all that I need. You are all I need.

FOR PERSONAL REFLECTION, PRAYER, AND STUDY

1. *Taking Out the Trash:* Read **Psalm 51:1–12; 2 Corinthians 7:1;** and **James 4:8–10.** Ask Christ to prepare your heart for His cleansing, purifying fire. Prayerfully take time to examine the unholy residue within your inner life; ask Him to show you anything that is hindering His life from fully occupying your heart and soul. Set aside a long period of time when you will not be distracted or interrupted so you can work through part 1 of the "Inner Sanctuary" section on www.authenticgirl.com.

2. *Kicking Out Other Lovers:* Read **Exodus 20:3; Matthew 6:24;** and **Luke 14:33;** and reread the paraphrase of **Luke 14:33** on page 63 of *Authentic Beauty.* Ask Christ to prepare you to let go of anything in your life that you are placing above Him. Prayerfully take time to examine the things that claim your affection, attention, time, and energy and distract you from intimacy with Christ. Set aside a long period of time when you will not be distracted or interrupted to prayerfully work through part 2 of the "Inner Sanctuary" section on www.authenticgirl.com.

OVERCOMING ROADBLOCKS

What about unconditional love?

After *Authentic Beauty* was released, I received an e-mail from a young woman who felt that "Taking Out the Trash" and "Kicking Out Other Lovers" was extreme and unnecessary. "I don't think it is necessary to go through some intense soul-searching process just to draw closer to God," she wrote. "He loves me just the way I am. I just need to receive that love."

I understand where this mind-set comes from. In today's modern Christian world, many of us have been told over and over again about God's unconditional love. We are told that He loves and accepts us just the way we are. Repentance, holiness, and making practical life changes are often looked down upon as legalistic. Previous generations focused intensely on obeying Christian rules in order to win God's favor and often had no personal relationship with Christ as a result. Their Christian faith became stale and lifeless. In response to the dead Christianity of generations past, our generation has swung to the opposite extreme: focusing on receiving God's unconditional love but not acknowledging His desire to make us holy.

But the gospel is more than receiving God's unconditional love. Yes, it is true that He loved and desired us even while we were dead in our sin. In fact, He loved us so much that He gave up everything in order to rescue us. But He didn't conquer sin and death on our behalf so that we could accept His forgiveness and then go on living sinful, self-focused lives. He came to purify us, cleanse us, and make us holy. (Read **Matthew 5:48; 1 Peter 1:16;** and **Romans 6:10–12, 19.**) He loves us as we are, yes. But He loves us far too much to leave us that way.

Think about a relationship between a husband and wife. Whenever I say or do something that hurts Eric (or vice versa), it creates a wall of distance and tension in our relationship. Our intimacy is hindered until the offense is dealt with. What if I simply shrugged if off and said, "I shouldn't have to make things right. Eric should love me the just way I am"? Would our romance thrive with that attitude?

When unresolved sin and unholy habits are allowed to remain in our lives, they *do* hurt God's heart, and they *do* hinder our intimacy with Him. (Read **Matthew 16:24** and **Revelation 3:15–16.**) Don't buy in to the common mind-set that intimacy with Christ does not require personal sacrifice. Be willing to remove whatever stands in the way. You will be amazed at the endless frontier of divine romance that awaits you.

What about legalism?

When going through a self-examination process, it is so important that we have the right foundation in place. We should not attempt to cleanse our lives out of a sense of duty or obligation. Our motives should not be to "appease God" or win brownie points in heaven. They should be out of intense love for our Lord and a desire to remove anything standing in the way of our intimacy with Him. The Christian life is not about rules; it is about a relationship. Unless a love relationship with Jesus Christ undergirds our motives for living set-apart lives, we will be governed by legalistic laws rather than the Spirit of Christ.

Amy Carmichael writes:

> It is not that Christ forbids us this or that comfort or indulgence; it is not that He is stern, demanding us to follow a narrow path. But we who love our Lord and whose affections are set on Heavenly things *voluntarily and gladly* lay aside the things that charm and ravish the world, so that our hearts may be ravished with the things of Heaven, that our whole being may be poured forth in constant and unreserved devotion in the service of the Lord who died to save us.[9]

Once you intimately know Jesus Christ, the way you live will have nothing to do with rules. Ask yourself why you want to make godly decisions and right choices. Is it because you love your Prince so much and desire to please Him in all you do, or is it because you are simply trying to stay on His "good side"? Ask Him to fill your heart with overwhelming love and desire for Him. The more you pursue intimacy with Him, the more you will naturally long to live for Him alone.

What does it mean to lay everything down?

As you go through the process of removing other lovers in your life, be aware that the Enemy of your soul is very clever. He may actually stroke you as you go through the cleansing process, encouraging you to lay *some* of your life at the feet of Jesus. But he will inevitably try to blind you from a few prized other lovers, whispering that you don't *really* need to let go of that relationship, that dream, that activity, or that pursuit you cherish the most. Read **1 Samuel 15:15–23** and **Acts 5:1–11**. What is God's perspective on giving Him *almost* everything that He asks us for?

Tearing Down Idols

(BY MEGAN, 21, NEBRASKA)

"She went after her lovers, and forgat me, saith the LORD.
(Hosea 2:13, KJV)

As I pulled my little white car into my driveway, I felt as if my life was coming to a screeching halt. It was a week before my twentieth birthday. Something was stirring within my heart. I reached for my cell phone, feeling that if I didn't get this off of my chest soon, I would explode. I hurriedly dialed my friend Jess's number. The conversation didn't get too far before I burst into tears and explained all that was going on in my heart and mind.

"I think I need to break up with him," I said as tears streamed down my face. Once again, I had given my heart to a guy and let it go way too far. Although nothing about the relationship was stable or God centered, I wanted to hold on to it. I had invested so much in this relationship—how could I possibly let it go?

But I knew the Lord was calling me to something else. It seemed as if God had taken His mighty wrecking ball and was smashing down all

I had held higher than Him. I was fearful of what was to come.

For several nights after that unforgettable day, I lay in bed and clung to my Bible, poring over the psalms. One night, trembling, I realized what I had made of the past twenty years of my life. What would become of the next twenty? I made the decision to take a season to focus on the Lord alone—not a job, not a boyfriend, not school, not my future. Him alone.

Days later, I was cleaning out the closet in my room. I had just spent the morning in prayer, asking the Lord to clean out my soul and all that hindered my relationship with Him. As I made my way through old school projects, notes from friends, and a mass of clothes and shoes, I found something unexpected: my journal from high school. I could hardly remember having this journal or ever writing anything in it! I glanced through its pages, and a piece of paper fell to the floor. On it was a prayer:

Dear heavenly Father,
Please help me to walk a straight walk only seeking Your will.
Lord, make my heart pure in all I do.

(continued on next page)

I also pray for my future husband. I pray that he would mature and grow spiritually as I do.

I know and trust You hear my prayers, Lord. Be with me now.

In Your precious name, amen.

The journal fell to the floor, and I was soon to follow. There on my knees, I didn't know what to do but cry out to the Lord. What had happened to that young girl? What had gone wrong?

My favorite verse in the Bible has always been Matthew 7:13–14: "Enter by the narrow gate; for wide is the gate and broad is the way that leads to destruction, and there are many who go in by it. Because narrow is the gate and difficult is the way which leads to life, and there are few who find it" (NKJV).

Now I found myself asking: how could a girl with such a sincere desire to follow the Lord have fallen so short? I had asked to walk a straight walk—I surely hadn't done that! I had asked the Lord to make my heart pure—I surely had not been pure!

I looked through the rest of the journal, and after about ten pages, the pages were blank. No more prayer, no more scripture. I had my answer. I had turned from the path of seeking Christ's ways to the path of seeking my own ways. I had allowed other lovers into my soul and become blind to any other way to live. I had thought of myself as a healthy Christian girl. But the truth was that in high school and my early years of college, it was popularity, cheerleading, friends, my boyfriend, and social nights on the weekends that claimed the highest place in my life. Time with Him fell into last place or no place. I said my prayers as I fell asleep at night and memorized scripture in my Bible class at the Christian school I attended, and that was the extent of my walk with Him.

I sat convicted. My life was meant for the glory of the Lord, and I had taken it and done as I had pleased with it. I longed to never let the same thing happen again.

Not long after that, I sat in my backyard and wrote in my journal:

I dedicate my life to know You more, Jesus. I am inviting You in. Move in to my life and change me to be like You! I give up everything to You as a sacrifice. I am Yours to use in any way. I give everything to You, Lord:

My life

My love life

(continued on next page)

My shopping habits

My social life

My family relationships

My job

My eating habits

My activities

My time

These are *all* Yours, not mine. Here they are, for You to have. Help me, Lord, to get rid of anything that does not bring glory to Your name!

And the Lord began to work in each of these areas—so faithfully, so tenderly.

My life… He took it completely into His hands, prying my fingers loose from the controls.

My love life… He led me to break up with my boyfriend, even in the middle of a serious relationship, and he put a deep desire within my heart to wait for my future husband before entering into another relationship again.

My shopping habits… I made the decision to stop buying clothes until I had clear direction of how to honor the Lord with my shopping habits. I even sold most of my clothes, which was a difficult decision, but looking back I learned so much through that process.

My social life… I began praying for like-minded friends and gave myself an early curfew so I could leave social events to go home and spend time with the Lord. This decision seemed very strange, but those were my favorite times of day.

My family relationships… In the past, I had lost my mom's trust. I began to pray for restoration in my relationship with her. The Lord beautifully restored what was broken between us.

My job… I left my all-consuming job for one that did not take my life's focus. Though it was a difficult decision, God provided for me in my new job and orchestrated beautiful relationships there.

My time… I learned that my time is not my time, it is God's time. I do not own a minute; they are all His. Daily, I prayed for my minutes to be used as He desired them to be.

The days when God took everything from my hands and placed them into His were painful. But what I remember most is His grace. He took my ashes and replaced them with His beauty. He knocked down all the idols I had placed on the altar of my soul and replaced them with His life.

How could I ever ask for more?

5

Beautiful Reflection

Shaping the Outward Lifestyle

*C*HRIST SAYS TO US, *"Stop trying to fit Me into your life. Instead,* build your life around Me." If we long for true intimacy with Him, it is not enough to prepare our inner environment for Him. We must also shape our outward lifestyle completely around Him.

OPENING UP

1. Today's culture assumes a lot about what activities and thoughts make a young woman "normal." Read the story of Peter and John in **Acts 4:33**. Were Jesus's followers considered normal? Who else in the Bible led atypical lives in order to follow God's leading?

We live in a constant tension between the urgent and the important. Many important tasks need not be done today, or even this week. Extra hours of prayer and Bible study, a visit to an elderly friend, reading an important book: these activities can usually wait a while longer. But often the urgent—though less important—tasks call for immediate response. The appeal of these urgent demands seems irresistible, and they devour our energy. But in the light of eternity their momentary prominence fades. With a sense of loss we recall the important tasks that have been shoved aside. We realize we have become slaves to the tyranny of the urgent.

CHARLES E. HUMMEL[10]

2. In what ways do you try to be normal, to fit into society and live the way others do? How does the idea of being "abnormal" make you feel?

> I don't care about being abnormal. Wouldn't do anything but draw my relationship w/ the Lord closer. A lot of the time people try to fit in with style and language.
> math
> modesty
> music
> movies
> morals

3. What is the difference between God's pace and the world's pace? Which pace does *your* life reflect? *Scripture suggestions:* **Psalm 23; Mark 1:35.**

> God's pace is God's timing. Careful and peaceful. The world is fast, outgoing and crazy. I reflect mostly God's pace. I try my hardest everyday. What is in the world's pace will soon be in God's as I strive to reach God's.

The Next Level

1. In what ways do you spend time on temporary, "urgent" things before eternal things? What is most likely to distract you from spending time with Christ? What practical changes might be needed in your life in order to shape your outward existence around intimacy with Him? *Scripture suggestion:* **Psalm 127:1.**

> my phone and the computer. & friends.
> give myself a certain time everyday to spend specially with God.
> * Just ask God to work in you to create a desire with him. Just spending time with him in general. Meditate on him throughout the day.

Living for an Audience of One
(BY GABRIELLE, 21, COLORADO)

For the past three years I've been living on a secular college campus. It is here that I have learned what it truly means to be set apart. Modern-day Christianity dictates that we should remain pure, but we shouldn't ostracize ourselves from society by becoming different. So Christians do whatever we can to remain "cool" while remaining technically "pure." We are told that that's the best way to reach out to others. But is that really true? It makes me wonder: Are we changing the world? Or is the world changing us?

I have learned that if I desire to live a life that is truly set apart, it is impossible to always please the crowd. I have decided to live my life for an audience of One.

I picture myself on a stage in front of a crowd. I am going about my day, and I look over to the left side of the crowd that is watching me. They are all smiling and clapping, and I feel accepted. But then I look over to the right, and I see the crowd there screaming and booing at my "performance." I feel discouraged and brokenhearted. Wasn't it my goal to please the crowd? I ask, *God, how can I ever live to please the crowd? How will I ever know what is the right thing to do?*

But he simply answers, *Look at Me.* I take another look into the crowd. There, in the front row, I see Jesus. I look into His face, so full of strength and peace and life—abundant life. And suddenly, I realize what it is I need to do. I need to live a life that pleases Him, the One who loves me more than any human being ever could.

So I begin to live again. Only this time, I live with only His desires in mind. At first I still notice the crowd with its boos and its cheers. It's hard not to be distracted, but I keep living for Him alone, sitting in the front row. Then one day, I look out into the crowd and I notice Jesus, only Jesus. The crowd has disappeared. I am left with my audience of One!

I had a friend who encouraged me to wake up each morning and pray this prayer: *Lord, today I give You my life. Do with me what You will. And if at the end of the day You are pleased, that's all that matters.* That simple prayer of devotion has revolutionized my life. The concept of living for an audience of One has changed the way I think and act. I still sometimes grapple with the need to please the crowd. But He is ever faithful to show me that He is always there sitting in the front row, smiling. And when I remember that, all I want to do is live for His pleasure.

2. It's easy to assume that doing a lot of Christian activities is equal to an active, personal relationship with Christ. Are you personally pursuing the fullness of all that Christ is, or are you settling for merely talking, singing, and reading about who He is? What changes might you need to make in your life in order for you to truly seek Him with all your heart, soul, mind, and strength? *Scripture suggestions:* **Deuteronomy 4:29; Psalm 42:1; Ephesians 3:17–19.**

   Need to thirst for him. We are desperate for him. all my heart, all my soul and all my mind. Realize how big those are.... This is who our God is.

3. On pages 79-82 of *Authentic Beauty*, I share the story of Amy Carmichael's life transformation. At the age of seventeen, she realized that she could not just say that she was Christ's follower; she needed to completely change her life in order to *become* Christ's follower. That is when she became "one of the few" in her generation and her life began to make an eternal impact on this world. Can you relate to Carmichael's story? Why or why not? What are your thoughts and fears about becoming "one of the few" in your generation?

FOR PERSONAL REFLECTION, PRAYER, AND STUDY

1. On pages 72-78 of *Authentic Beauty*, I list three cultural assumptions that influenced my daily life. Prayerfully think through each of these three assumptions in relation to your own life, and ask God to align your perspective with His in these areas if needed:

   ASSUMPTION #1: *To be well adjusted and healthy, a young woman must have plenty of friends her own age and must spend a large amount of her time and energy maintaining those friendships.*

   Examine the friendships in your life. Read **John 15:12–17** and **James 4:4**. Which friendships truly glorify Christ, showcase His love, and lead you closer to Him? Which friendships are simply there to elevate your popularity status or make you feel more secure? Are there friendships in your life that pull you further away from God's kingdom? What practical changes might you need to make in this area of your life in order to shape your existence around Christ?

   abbey
   Kyle
   connor
   steph
   Britt
   Corin
   Dan
   There are friends that pull me away.
   pray for my friends. Maybe back off
   a little from my non christian friends.
   Give it to God.

ASSUMPTION #2: *To have a successful future, a young woman must carefully follow society's pattern for success.*

Examine your future plans and ambitions. Read **1 Timothy 6:17–18; Hebrews 13:5; and 1 John 2:15–17.** Are you making life decisions based on worldly expectations or selfish ambition? If so, what practical changes can you make in that area to shape your life around Christ?

I do not think I am making life decisions based on worldly expectation. I follow my heart and live for God.

ASSUMPTION #3: *To find true love, a young woman must put a huge amount of effort into pursuing romantic relationships.*

"...all the days of our lives..."

Examine your focus on romance and relationships. Read **Proverbs 31:12** and **1 Corinthians 7:34a.** What should your primary focus be while you are single? How do your thoughts, energy, and use of time reflect or contradict that focus? How do you respond to the idea of trusting God to take control of this area of your life? What practical changes might you need to make in this area of your life to shape your existence around Christ?

To please the Lord. I need to put complete trust in the Lord and think about pleasing him in every possible way.

2. Ask God to show you any other wrong assumptions that control your daily life. Ask Him to show you what practical changes you must make in order to shape your outward lifestyle around Him alone. Write down what He is speaking to your heart.

OVERCOMING ROADBLOCKS

What about dreams and desires?

It is easy to become worried that, once we shape our existence around Jesus Christ, we will never see any of our own dreams or desires fulfilled. As Elisabeth Elliot writes, "God's primary concern is not for us to be happy, but to be holy."[11] But ironically, it is only when we truly pursue Christ and live a life fully consecrated to His glory that *we find true happiness and fulfillment.* As Matthew 6:19–21 declares, any other pursuit will only fade into nothingness in the end. He is all that truly matters. I love Psalm 16:11: "In Your presence is fullness of joy; In Your right hand there are pleasures forever." Yes, God wants us to have dreams and desires for our lives, but not our own dreams…*His* dreams for us.

FINDING YOUR LIFE'S PURPOSE

It started a few months before I graduated from high school. The constant questions, the offhanded suggestions, the palpable pressure to figure out my life. "So where are you going to college?" friends and family asked. "Have you looked into any missionary programs yet?" others prodded. "You should really think about doing a year or two of overseas outreach work!"

My stack of university brochures rivaled the collection of the most overeager college fair attendee. My list of Bible schools and missions programs was longer than a nationwide record of SAT scores. But I still didn't have a clue what I was supposed to do with my life. I prayed. I sought counsel from people I respected. I attended seminars on finding purpose. I read books on decision making. I prayed some more. In spite of my relentless searching, my life's direction still seemed as elusive as a desert mirage. Who was I? What was the meaning of my life? Why couldn't I grasp God's plan for my future?

I received advice from many different perspectives. My youth pastor's opinion was simple. "Follow your heart!" he proclaimed passionately. "God wants you to be happy. Make decisions based on what feels right." But every time I followed my heart and kept God out of it, I ended up making terrible decisions.

My longtime mentor offered an interesting solution. "Take a detailed personality test. Only when you understand your unique psychological profile can you make wise life decisions." But after a six-hour personality test, I was no closer to a solution than I'd been before.

More confused than ever, I turned to a respected older pastor for counsel.

"God doesn't have a specific plan for your life," he declared after hearing my dilemma, "so stop waiting for a heavenly revelation. God just wants you to live morally and use your common sense. Just make your own decisions and He will bless them." But I had seen God put the details of my life together so many times that I couldn't believe He wanted me to figure things out on my own.

I became intensely frustrated with God. Didn't He understand that I had decisions to make? Didn't He realize that I was running out of time?

Then one day I stumbled upon the story of Dr. Walter Wilson, a respected Christian physician in the early 1900s. Several years into his life as a Christian, Dr. Wilson became severely discouraged. He had no clear sense of purpose. He had no sense of God's presence. He didn't feel that his life's work was producing significant results. One night, after hearing a challenging message at church, he went home and fell on his face before God. *My Lord,* he said brokenly, *I have mistreated You all my life. I have treated You like a servant. When I wanted You, I called for You; when I was about to engage in something important, I beckoned You to come and help me perform my task. I have sought to use You only as a servant to help me in my self-appointed work. I will do so no more.*[12]

Wilson's prayer of repentance pierced my soul. I realized that I, too, was guilty of treating God like a servant. I had come before Him time and time again, expecting Him to provide me with a solution, demanding that He meet my needs and follow my self-made agenda. When He didn't respond, I had dismissed Him and taken matters into my own hands.

(continued on next page)

treating God like a servant. Unselfishly spend time with him.

With tears of remorse streaming down my face, I knelt beside my bed. I read the second half of Dr. Wilson's heart-wrenching prayer and prayed the words right along with him. *Lord, I give You this body of mine; from my head to my feet, I give it to You. My hands, my limbs, my eyes, my brain; all that I am inside and out, I hand over to You. Live in and through me whatever life You please. You may send this body to Africa, or lay it on a bed with cancer. You may blind my eyes, or send me with Your message to Tibet. You may take this body to the Eskimos, or send it to a hospital with pneumonia. This body of mine is Yours alone from this moment on.*

That prayer was the answer to all my deepest questions. It was heaven's response to the mystery of my life's purpose. Suddenly, it didn't seem important where I went to college, or whether I did missions work instead. It didn't seem to matter when I got married, what career I pursued, or what my five-year plan was supposed to be. My life was no longer my own. My body was merely a shell that housed the Spirit of almighty God. And He could live His life through me exactly as He chose.

That day, I took the first step toward a God-written life story. That day, I realized that the purpose of my life did not revolve around pursuing my own desires, making my own plans, or following my own dreams. The purpose of my life revolved around Him—knowing Him, loving Him, pursuing more of Him. I was no longer driven to figure out who I was. It only mattered who He was. I began to let go of my own agenda. I began to be at peace with not knowing the future, trusting God to put the pieces together in His own perfect way. This wasn't my life to live—it was His.

The Author of true life took the pen and began scripting the details of my existence. And that's when my life truly began. It is not that I have never taken the pen back out of His hands to write my own story—far from it! It is not that I never again struggled with finding my purpose or making decisions. But that day, I embarked upon the ultimate adventure, the adventure of a God-scripted life. And I have never regretted it for a moment.

Over the past several years, Eric and I have been bombarded with life-purpose questions from our generation: "How do I figure out what college God wants me to attend?" "How do I know if God wants me to stay in this relationship?" "How do I launch into full-time ministry?" When we tell young adults to give God the pen and allow Him to write their life stories, we are often met with impatient frowns and frustrated sighs.

"Yes, I've already done that," is a typical response, "but now I really need to make some decisions! I've got to figure out what to do!" During key decision-making seasons of life, we long for a step-by-step guide to making the right choices in relationships, education, and career. All too often, we offer the pen of our lives to God and then become impatient when He doesn't immediately make our paths clear.

It is true that God can use our desires or common sense to help lead us in the right direction. When we rely on our own desires, our own intelligence, or the advice of "experts," we might even be able to write our own life stories in ways that we appear successful to those around us. But until the Author of true life scripts every aspect our existence—not in theory, but in our day-to-day reality—we cannot truly live. Choosing to give God the pen of our lives is not just a one-time prayer that produces instant answers to all of life's dilemmas. It is a lifestyle.

6

Lily Whiteness and Romance

Future Husband Application

$\mathcal{O}$NLY WHEN WE fall in love with our true Prince, Jesus Christ, and build our lives around Him can we experience love and romance in their purest and most beautiful forms. The first step to finding a God-written love story begins with our handing the pen to the true Author of romance. Remember, He cares more about this area of your life than even you do—and He will take very good care of the things that you entrust to Him.

OPENING UP

1. What if your future husband could see your actions and thoughts toward the opposite sex? Would he feel honored and cherished? Or would he feel hurt and jealous? What changes might you need to make in this area of your life in order to love your future husband all the days of your life?

   He would feel hurt and jealous. Live purely. Honoring God through any action.
   Only marry 1 person. the one God wants/ has in store for you.
   what kind of vibe to I have to people I meet?

2. It is tempting to think of our single years as just a waiting period before we get married and our "real" lives begin. But if we place all our hopes and expectations in a human romance, we will be disappointed. Read **John 4:13–14.** Christ's love is the only love that satisfies us eternally. In what ways do you look to an earthly love story (or the hope of one) to satisfy your soul?

   through holding hands, hugging, cuddling, kissing...

Honeymoon Love Letters

(EXCERPT FROM *WHEN GOD WRITES YOUR LOVE STORY*)

Eric's face was alight with boyish excitement as he reached into a suitcase and pulled out a huge spiral notebook. "I have something I want to show you, Les," he said, a smile playing on his lips.

It was our honeymoon—by far the most incredible two weeks of my life. After waiting for what seemed like an eternity, I was finally Mrs. Eric Ludy! And just when I thought I had discovered the depth of Eric's love for me, he took it to yet a deeper level.

"See all these letters?" he said, flipping through page after page of notebook paper. "I wrote these to you years before we ever met. I've been saving them for our honeymoon!"

Though the letters were not addressed to me, they may as well have had my name on them. Each one, in its unique way, told of Eric's unfailing love and devotion to the woman who would one day share his life with him. His faithfulness to me before we met gave me amazing security in our marriage.[13]

THE NEXT LEVEL

1. Have you had past relationships that were not honoring to your future spouse? How did those relationships affect your intimate relationship with Jesus Christ?

   Never had one

2. In what ways does the culture (even the Christian culture) pressure you to lower your standards for set-apartness and true purity? What people and places might you need to avoid in order to remain strong in your commitment to a Christ-centered relationship? *Scripture suggestions:* **Psalm 57:2–3; 1 Thessalonians 2:4.**

   I need to avoid my friends who are not a good influence on me; whether they be in a relationship or not.

3. How can you allow your desire for earthly love to deepen your depend-
   ence upon Christ? *Scripture suggestions:* **Psalm 27:14; 103:5; Song of
   Solomon 8:4.**

   Have more trust in the Lord

THE BEAUTY OF SET-APARTNESS

Many generations ago, there lived a sweet and soft-hearted young woman
named Sarah. At a very young age, she surrendered her existence to Jesus
Christ. He transformed her with His stunning radiance and purity. As a
young teenager, while other girls were focused on finding husbands, Sarah
was focused entirely on her romance with her Prince. And as she found her
satisfaction and fulfillment in Him, she sparkled with a radiance that caused
others to stand back in awe. The following description was written about
Sarah by the godly young man who would one day become her husband:

> They say there is a young lady in New Haven who is beloved of
> that Great Being who made and rules the world. They say that He
> fills her mind with exceeding sweet delight, and that she hardly

(continued on next page)

FOR PERSONAL REFLECTION, PRAYER, AND STUDY

1. When you choose to be set apart for your future husband, it is a great idea to put your commitment in writing and refer to it during times of doubt, temptation, or loneliness. In your own words, express how you desire to live for your future husband from this day forward.

I want him to see my difference to others in the world to please him to be the way God is for me.

cares for anything except to meditate on Him. If you present all the world to her, with the richest of its treasures, she disregards it. She is unmindful of any pain or affliction. She has a singular purity in her affections. You could not persuade her to compromise her true Love even if you would give her all the world. She possesses a wonderful sweetness, calmness, and kindness to those around her. She will sometimes go about from place to place, singing sweetly. She seems to be always full of joy and pleasure, and no one knows exactly why. She loves to be alone, walking in the fields and groves, and seems to have Someone invisible always conversing with her.[14]

Sarah's future husband was enthralled by her all-consuming love for

2. If you have made mistakes in the area of relationships, take some time to bring your sin before God and let Him restore you. Make a decision to turn and go the opposite direction from your sin. Take a moment to put your commitment in writing.

I dont think i have...

Jesus. It was not worldly allure or charm that captivated the heart of her Warrior Poet. It was the spectacular loveliness of Christ flowing through her.

I've seen a similar story played out more recently. My friend Nicole is a set-apart young woman who won the heart of a wonderful, godly guy. The first time he sent her flowers, he did not send something traditional, like roses. He sent her a single lily surrounded by thorns, with a card that read, "Like a lily among thorns, so is my darling among the maidens" (see Song of Solomon 2:2). Christ had shaped Nicole into a radiant lily among thorns. It was her Christlike set-apartness that captivated the heart of her earthly prince.

Remember, a truly Christ-built man won't be drawn to you through feminine manipulation, flirting, or flaunting. Instead, his heart will be ravished by the stunning radiance and set-apartness that flows from your life.

3. Remember, once you have repented of your sin, God forgives you completely. When He looks at you, He doesn't see even a trace of that sin anymore. Read **Exodus 15:13; Psalm 33:18; Ephesians 3:17–19;** and **1 Peter 4:8;** and ask God to show you how He sees you. Write down what He is speaking to your heart.

4. If you learn to be a one-man woman with your physical body, your mind, and your affections, you set the stage for an earthly love story that is out of this world. What most excites you about this journey with Christ? What dreams has He placed in your heart for this area of your life?

   The love my husband will give me, how he'll love me despite my mistakes. He's made me dream of what kind of man God has in store for me. This excites me and encourages me all the more to be a lilly among thorns.

One True Lover

(BY KENDRA, 21, PENNSYLVANIA)

My story is a typical one. I was raised in a Christian family, loved the Lord, loved popularity, and loved the boy who stole my heart at age fourteen. We enjoyed the same activities, had compatible personalities, and were living lives headed in the same direction. What a dream! Our friendship flourished into boyfriend-girlfriend. Our lives through high school were simple: we each had big circles of friends, spent as much time together as we could, and enjoyed all God had blessed us with.

But in so many ways we were a typical Christian dating couple, trying to live as close to the line as possible. We went to church every week and appeared healthy and spiritual to our youth group. But privately, though we maintained our abstinence commitment, we were compromising our physical purity. We attended parties where the crowd was definitely not honoring Christ. We wanted to honor God, but we were living for ourselves.

College proved to be an interesting time in our story. Bobby headed off to Wake Forest in North Carolina, and I attended a small school near our hometown. It was the first time we were separated for more than a few weeks, and frankly, I wasn't quite sure what to do with myself. Bobby had always been there. And now he wasn't. So began my journey to finding the fullness of Jesus Christ.

(continued on next page)

Without Bobby close by, I found myself turning to One who loved me more than I could ever ask. I needed to "taste and see that the LORD is good" (Psalm 34:8) and discover that He surpassed all my deepest longings. I had looked to Bobby to fill my desires, but now I understood that Bobby would never be enough. The Creator of the universe had placed in me a longing for eternal love, and He would be the only Person who could satisfy me. Deep down I had known this to be true. But when you meet a charming, handsome man of God, it can be easy to let him replace your heavenly Prince.

The process of putting Christ first in my life was not easy, but it was indescribably rewarding. As I began to draw near to Christ, He drew near to me. He rained His unconditional love down upon my life, and I was enthralled. Yet after days of wooing, He gently began to lead me into something I was deathly afraid of: the surrender of Bobby and the relationship I had poured myself into for five years.

I had a choice to make. To know Christ and all that He had for me, I knew I had to surrender Bobby, the man I felt I'd been given by God Himself, the person I planned to marry and spend the rest of my life with. It pierced me to the core. But how sweet and gentle my Prince was as I followed His lead to lay Bobby on the altar! He embraced my tear-stained face and whispered promises of unfailing love, unexplainable peace, and unabated joy in Him—forever.

God did amazing things in my heart, and I came to a place of complete fulfillment in Him. As I obeyed His voice in my life (which was terribly hard sometimes), He began to script out a story I couldn't have imagined. I was blessed with a beautiful, God-centered relationship with…Bobby. After I laid that relationship down at Christ's feet, He gave it back to me in His own perfect time and way. He turned what was once an unhealthy, proud, idolatrous relationship into a wonderful and radiant display of Christ-centered love.

Bobby and I are now seeking Christ as our first love, and we are blessed beyond words that God would give us the gift of each other. I am in awe of the transformation Christ brought in our lives and our relationship. Just this past weekend, Bobby and I got engaged. Although this gift of Bobby is something that brings me great joy, every morning I surrender Bobby back to Christ. God recently showed me that I will be doing this for the rest of my life. Even after our wedding day, I must continue to relinquish my grasp on him. The Lord is good, and He will never change. So come what may, I will enjoy the gift of Bobby in my life for however long God has him or me on this earth. God's promise in Psalm 37:4 is something I am reminded of each morning I wake up: as I delight myself in *Him,* the desires of my heart will be met.

I beg you to believe and walk in this truth: God wants the very best for you and for me. We cannot lie to ourselves about relationships we're in, no matter how great they may seem. If God blesses you with a love story on this earth, it will be an amazing reflection of His burning passion, desire, and love for you, His lily, His bride! Don't settle for less.

OVERCOMING ROADBLOCKS

What if I am already in a relationship?

If God has been using this study to reshape your thinking in this area of your life and you are currently in a romantic relationship, most likely you are now wondering what to do. Does surrendering this area of your life to Christ mean that you should end your current relationship? Only God knows your heart and your individual situation. But let me offer you a few points to ponder.

The best way to determine if something has an unhealthy hold over your heart is to evaluate your willingness to let it go. If you find that the thought of losing this relationship is making you unwilling to give it up, the relationship has probably taken too strong a hold on your heart. Remember, even a God-written love story must be held loosely. As Job 1:21 says, "The LORD gives and the LORD takes away; blessed be the name of the LORD" (NEB).

Here is something that Eric and I often suggest to young people who are trying to evaluate a relationship. Take a season *away* from the relationship—for as long as it takes in order to truly gain God's direction and clarity. Yes, it may feel like a risky thing to do, but *nothing* is more important than placing God in His rightful place in your heart and life. During the time apart, don't talk on the phone, e-mail, or spend time together in person. Instead, spend your free time seeking God's direction for the relationship. When you are constantly spending time with your significant other, your emotions and human desires can easily get in the way and drown out God's still, small voice. Seek the counsel of godly older teammates (such as parents and spiritual leaders). If your parents are against the relationship, take their concern seriously. It may be God's way of giving you caution where caution is needed.

Remember that if God wants you to be in this relationship, He is capable of holding it together; it's not something that you have to control or manipulate. He will hold it safely in the palm of His hands. Your only job is to trust Him with all your heart, soul, mind, and strength. If you feel worried or anxious, read **Proverbs 3:5–6** and remember that His ways are perfect. Allow God to show you *His* desires for this area of your life. It may be the right relationship but the wrong time. Or it may not be the right relationship at all—be willing to hold out for God's very best. He cares more about this area of your life than even you do.

A Vision of Warrior Poets

1. Have you been discouraged or disgusted by the state of modern manhood? What would you like to see change when it comes to today's guys?

   I would like to see them dressed in a more modest way
   to see them talk more politely, have respect and
   to show you're a christian if you are one.. guys hide that.

2. In your own words, what is a Warrior Poet? What kind of man does God want you to wait for?

   One who is secking God, calling upon him all the time,
   has respect, is polite, sees me for who I really am and
   will forgive me through any situation.

3. How can you begin shaping the guys in your life into Warrior
   Poets? (Don't forget about dads and brothers! Consider giving your
   future sister-in-law an early wedding present by helping shape your
   brother into a heroic prince.) What are some practical ways that
   you can begin investing Christ's message into guys' lives, starting
   today? Remember, even though you might not see a guy change
   overnight, your consistent, Christlike example *will* make an
   impact, so don't give up!

   send/give them cards with a bible verse in it.
   Invite them to church/youth group / bible study...

romantic *mystique*

the mystery
of a set-apart
young woman

My beloved is mine and I am his;
he delights in the lilies.

Song of Songs 2:16, NEB

7

Feminine Mystique

Discovering the Lost Art of Mystery

*F*EMININE MYSTIQUE means valuing the things that God values. It is the dignity, confidence, strength, and purity that come from protecting our inner sanctuary and guarding our intimacy with Christ above all else.

OPENING UP

1. In her book *A Return to Modesty*, Wendy Shalit writes:

   In my freshman year at college I told my dorm-mates that I didn't much care for the idea of sharing a bathroom with male students. Immediately one of the girls smiled condescendingly and wrapped her arm around my shoulder, explaining that she, too, once thought that she wouldn't like coed bathrooms, but then, she said, "I became comfortable with my body." (She implied that) someday I would learn to put away childish things (like modesty).[15]

   In what ways do you see this kind of attitude in the world around you? Has the culture pressured you to ignore your natural, God-given desire to guard your modesty and mystique? If so, how?

   hasn't pressured me but I see my friends dressing more revealing and boys dressing with their pants down to their knees...

2. What is missing from many modern Christians' approach to purity? What do you think is needed for an earthly romance to be truly beautiful and God-honoring and not just technically pure?

   The romance has to be based on God and all about him, we need to read, listen and apply what pure is in God's eyes.

3. It is all too easy for us to give ourselves to guys emotionally, as Sarah on page 116 of *Authentic Beauty* did. Has this been a struggle in your own life? Why is it dangerous to give yourself emotionally to someone without a God-centered commitment of marriage? *Scripture suggestions:* **Proverbs 4:23; Song of Solomon 8:4.**

Because you're giving your heart away. It's like taking the fence down.

Teach me, my Lord, to be sweet and gentle in all the events of life, in disappointments, in the thoughtlessness of others, in the insincerity of those I trusted, in the unfaithfulness of those on whom I relied. Let me put myself aside, to think of the happiness of others, to hide my little pains and heartaches, so that I may be the only one to suffer from them. Teach me to profit by the suffering that comes across my path. Let me so use it that it may mellow me, not harden or embitter me; that it may make me broad in my forgiveness, [kindly, sympathetic, and helpful].

UNKNOWN AUTHOR[16]

THE NEXT LEVEL

1. Are you willing to protect your heart for your one true King, even when the world around you is screaming at you to compromise? What does it mean to protect the sacred things in your life?

   Yes. To protect the sacred things in your life means to protect the special, holey, Godly things God placed in there for you & you only.

2. What are some practical things you can do to protect your sanctuary and guard intimacy with your Prince? (Optional: Write out your personal commitment in your own words.)

   Not let boys become number one in my life. stay away, dress modestly

FOR PERSONAL REFLECTION, PRAYER, AND STUDY

Let's look at some of the most common compromises that young women face. Prayerfully ponder each one of these areas in relationship to your own life, and ask God to purify you and change your habits wherever needed.

Gossip: Read **Leviticus 19:16** and **Proverbs 16:28**. The Bible is clear about gossip (which is also called *slander* in the Bible). Carefully examine the way you speak about others. Have you fallen into the sin of gossip or slander? Has it become a habit in your life? In what practical ways can you begin to honor God in this area?

i speak in a very positive way about my friends. I will speak to my friends as if I'm talking to God.

Selfishness: Read **Acts 20:24** and **Philippians 3:8**. In our modern culture, we are bombarded with messages that tell us to consider ourselves first. Christ wants to teach us how to put Him and others far above ourselves. Carefully examine the focus of your daily existence. Do you habitually put yourself first? Write down any specific ways in which you are selfish. Think: does your selfishness affect anyone else? If it does, perhaps you need to ask for forgiveness from those people. If it does not, it still hurts God and hinders your intimacy with Him. In what practical ways can you begin to honor God in this area?

No, I don't normally put myself first.

Materialism: Read **Matthew 19:16–22** and **Luke 12:15–21**. Jesus spoke very clearly about how the pursuit of and preoccupation with worldly possessions and wealth can keep us from discovering the kingdom of heaven. Prayerfully ask God to show you the difference between your needs and your wants. How much of your time and energy is devoted to pursuing selfish, temporary, material things? In what practical ways can you begin to honor God in this area? (A great way to determine whether your possessions or financial pursuits have an unhealthy hold over your heart is to ask yourself if you are willing to give them up.)

Laziness: Read **Proverbs 6:6–11; 10:4**. We are often lazy and do not even realize it, especially when it comes to cultivating our intimacy with Christ or making sacrifices for others. We justify studying hard because we believe it will one day give us a good job with a good salary. But why is it so difficult to put any effort into our relationship with God? God asks us to be disciplined when it comes to growing in our faith. He asks us to be sacrificial and willing to serve others. In what practical ways can you begin to honor God in this area?

Self-Pity: Read **Psalm 143:7–11** and **1 Corinthians 7:30–31.** It is normal to feel sad or lonely at times, especially when living a set-apart life that others often don't understand. But wallowing in our own misfortunes and allowing ourselves to inwardly moan and groan about every outward struggle we face is extremely dangerous. Self-pity blinds us to the needs of others and keeps us focused on ourselves

"The time has arrived for pruning the vines,…
Arise, my darling, my beautiful one,
And come along!"
O my dove, in the clefts of the rock,
In the secret place of the steep pathway,
Let me see your form,
Let me hear your voice;
For your voice is sweet,
And your form is lovely. (Song of Solomon 2:12–14)

Life Meaning: To experience the depth and beauty of intimacy with Christ, we must allow Him to prune us and make us like Him. Intimacy is not cultivated on the easy path but in the secret place of the steep path. We become beautiful as we allow Him to shape us, to lead us where others won't dare to venture.

and not our Prince. James 1:2–4 tells us to consider it pure joy when we are faced with various trials, so that the testing of our faith can produce patience, making us mature and complete. Carefully examine the way you handle life's challenges. Do you allow trials to draw you closer to Christ? Or do you always give in to anger, depression, and hopelessness? Ask God to show you how He wants you to respond to trials. Write down what He is speaking to your heart.

OVERCOMING ROADBLOCKS

How do I protect my mystique if I have an outgoing personality?

Feminine mystique is not about withdrawing from guy friendships or suppressing an outgoing nature. It is about guarding the parts of you that are meant only for Christ and for your future husband. For instance, if you are offering hugs and flirtatious touches that could be interpreted as sensual, you are giving away affection that is only meant for your future spouse, not to mention possibly creating temptation for the guys. If you are opening your heart and sharing your most intimate dreams, desires, and fears with guys, you are giving away intimacy and emotions that were meant only for your husband.

It is definitely possible to guard feminine mystique even when you have a friendly and outgoing personality. You can be friendly without being flirtatious. You can be outgoing without offering your emotions and affection to the guys you interact with. Prayerfully ask God to show you any ways in which you are allowing your mystique to be compromised. He will be faithful to gently direct your steps and make you into a woman of mystery, no matter what your personality.

How quickly should I open my heart to a guy I'm interested in?

God designed us as women to be pursued by men, not the other way around. He designed us to respond slowly, not quickly, to a man's romantic initiation. Our hearts and our love should only be given once a future spouse has "won" us in a Christlike way. They should not be offered for the taking right in the very beginning. They should be treated as precious treasures, offered only to the one who is worthy of that gift. The entire book of Song of Solomon illustrates this principle. It showcases a bridegroom pursuing the heart of his beloved and the bride responding and opening her heart to him gradually, in love's perfect timing. Don't let your impatience cause you to miss out on the beauty of a bridegroom winning the heart of his bride—it's God's perfect pattern.

In *Passion and Purity,* Elisabeth Elliot writes of her blossoming love story with Jim, her future husband, and paints a beautiful example of feminine mystique:

> Waiting silently is the hardest thing of all. I was dying to talk to Jim and about Jim. But the things we feel most deeply we ought to learn to be silent about, at least until we have talked them over thoroughly with God. Three days before my graduation, Jim and I spent the afternoon in a little park…. We talked very little, enjoyed the sun, flowers, lake, birds, and insects. My heart was full to bursting with things I wanted to say (things like, "I love you, I can't live without you," and all the desperate phrases women always want to say). I am sure it was good for me to refrain. God's time for further revelations of the heart might come later.

Tomorrow was not our business; it was His. Letting it rest with Him was the discipline of the day, and it was enough.[17]

How do I guard my heart when I am attracted to a guy?

Being attracted to someone is not wrong; it's what you do with that attraction that matters. When attraction begins to control your thoughts and emotions, that's when it becomes dangerous. So develop the discipline of constantly surrendering your heart and emotions back to God. When you feel tempted to obsess about a certain guy, pray for him instead, and then train your mind to meditate on Scripture or pray for an unsaved loved one rather than fantasize about a relationship. Don't let your mind control you; take control of your mind and focus it on Jesus Christ. Don't let your emotions rule you; allow the Spirit of Jesus Christ to rule your emotions. If you build your life around Christ, He will show you when the time is right to open your heart to someone. Until then, make Him the love of your life, and He will be faithful to hold your heart in His hands.

Battle Secrets

Winning the War Against Compromise

*I*T'S EASY TO ASSUME that compromise catches us off guard and that falling into sin happens unexpectedly in our lives. But the reality is that every moment of every day, we are either on a path of light or on a path of darkness; we are either yielding to our selfish, sinful desires or we are yielding to the Spirit of Jesus Christ.

OPENING UP

1. Much of the American Christian culture has developed a careless attitude toward sin. What are some of the sins today's Christians treat carelessly? What kind of attitude does God want us to have toward sin? *Scripture suggestions:* **Ephesians 5:3–10; Colossians 3:5–8.**

   stealing, murder, lying, getting drunk, perverticy, movies, language
   God wants us to be cautious of sin and to get rid of them.

2. "A pure heart," says Johannes Tauler, "is one to which all that is not of God is strange and jarring."[18] Are ungodly things strange and jarring to you, or have you become lax and careless toward sin and impurity? Are there any sins that you have a careless attitude toward? (For example, do you shrug off the immorality in ungodly movies and television shows and watch them anyway? Do you laugh at crude jokes and sexual banter? Do you casually listen to or participate in gossip?) How might God want to change your attitude toward sin in your own life and sin in the world around you? *Scripture suggestions:* **Hebrews 12:1; 1 John 3:9.**

   God wants me to guard myself and know when I'm getting into trouble.
   Have someone to encourage you + be by yourside.

THE NEXT LEVEL

1. It is a myth that we suddenly "fall into sin" without warning. We begin on the path toward sin *the moment we give into temptation* and allow it to take root within our souls. In what areas of your life have you given into temptation and allowed it to take root within your soul? *Scripture suggestion:* **James 1:14–15.**

   I haven't...

2. Think back to Clare on pages 129–132 of *Authentic Beauty*. How is her story similar to or different from your own life? What most often causes you to fantasize about sinful things? How can you avoid that situation or thought pattern in the future?

   T.V., friends
   watch who I hang out with and what movies/T.V shows I watch

CALLED TO A HIGHER KINGDOM

Sophie is a college freshman who told me about a recent struggle in her relationship with Christ.

"All my life I dreamed of being in a sorority," she confessed. "But when I finally got into one, I noticed that the conversations and attitudes of the other girls were the opposite of Christlike. The girls were completely preoccupied with worldly things. And I found that I was becoming preoccupied with all the same things."

Sophie had a difficult decision to make. Should she walk away from her dream just because the sorority made it more difficult for her to focus on Christ? Other Christians in her life said she was being extreme. "Being a part of a sorority is an experience you'll never forget," they told her. "Why would you give it up? All the preoccupation with guys and clothes and parties is just harmless fun. You only go to college once! And besides, think of the great witness for Christ you can be in that environment."

But when Sophie listened to the voice of her Prince, He spoke a different message. He softly beckoned her to come away with Him.

"I went back and forth about it for weeks," she admitted. "But I finally realized that nothing in the world is worth jeopardizing my relationship with Christ. A sorority lasts for a couple years. My relationship with Christ is the most precious and valuable part of my life—it's the only thing that matters—and it lasts for eternity. So I walked away. It made no sense to anyone else. But now, I am closer to Him than I ever dreamed possible. Before, He was just a part of my life. Now, He is my life."

Amy Carmichael wrote:

> We must look upon the world, in all its delights and attractions, suspecting that traps are set for us there, and reserve ourselves for a higher way. The world is not for us. We are called to live daily in a higher Kingdom, where our souls drink from the Spirit of God.[19]

We each have our own "sororities"—dreams, activities, or pastimes that distract us from our one true love. Jesus Christ asks us if we, like Sophie, are willing to walk away from those things—to leave them far behind—and ride off into the sunset in the arms of our precious Prince.

3. On pages 145–148 of *Authentic Beauty,* I share the true story of a young woman named Esther Ahn Kim who chose to honor God even when it meant persecution and prison. In what ways might you be persecuted for your set-apart life? How do you respond to Esther Ahn Kim's bold actions to follow Christ? What is your heart's response to God's call to be one of the few who live for Him?

I am proud of her. A lot of ppl wouldn't do something like that because of other ppls reaction to what she did... I would have done what esther did.

FOR PERSONAL REFLECTION, PRAYER, AND STUDY

1. Read **1 Corinthians 6:18** and **2 Timothy 2:22**. God asks us not to walk away from sin but to *flee* from it. Prayerfully think through the sins you most often deal with in your own life, and allow God to show you what practical steps you need to take to physically flee from those things. Write down your personal strategy for how you plan to respond the next time you are faced with temptation. Are you willing to do whatever it takes to flee from temptation, even if it means walking out of a movie, a conversation, an activity, or a relationship?

2. Read **2 Corinthians 10:5** and **James 4:7**. Satan bombards us with the temptation of ungodly thoughts or lies. God asks us to *actively resist* the Enemy's tactics. Ask God to equip you to take every thought captive and respond to lies by filling your mind with His truth. Write down your own personal strategy for attacking lies with truth.

3. Read **Philippians 4:8**. A great way to start filling your mind with things that are lovely, pure, and right is by memorizing and meditating on one of the psalms—and letting your mind dwell on those heavenly words whenever you are attacked by lies. Psalm 27 (below) is one of my favorites. This week, read through this psalm every day (or choose your own) and meditate on its truth. You might want to consider memorizing some or part of this scripture in order to be ready with truth the next time mental temptation comes.

> The LORD is my light and my salvation—
>> whom shall I fear?
> The LORD is the stronghold of my life—
>> of whom shall I be afraid?
> When evil men advance against me
>> to devour my flesh,

when my enemies and my foes attack me,
   they will stumble and fall.
Though an army besiege me,
   my heart will not fear;
though war break out against me,
   even then will I be confident.

One thing I ask of the LORD,
   this is what I seek:
that I may dwell in the house of the LORD
   all the days of my life,
to gaze upon the beauty of the LORD
   and to seek him in his temple.
For in the day of trouble
   he will keep me safe in his dwelling;
he will hide me in the shelter of his tabernacle
   and set me high upon a rock.
Then my head will be exalted
   above the enemies who surround me;
at his tabernacle will I sacrifice with shouts of joy;
   I will sing and make music to the LORD.

Hear my voice when I call, O LORD;
   be merciful to me and answer me.
My heart says of you, "Seek his face!"
   Your face, LORD, I will seek.
Do not hide your face from me,
   do not turn your servant away in anger;

you have been my helper.
Do not reject me or forsake me,
  O God my Savior.
Though my father and mother forsake me,
  the LORD will receive me.
Teach me your way, O LORD;
  lead me in a straight path
  because of my oppressors.
Do not turn me over to the desire of my foes,
  for false witnesses rise up against me,
  breathing out violence.

I am still confident of this:
  I will see the goodness of the LORD
  in the land of the living.
Wait for the LORD;
  be strong and take heart
  and wait for the LORD. (Psalm 27:1–14, NIV)

4. Another great way to fight the attacks of the Enemy is to begin praying for an unsaved loved one the moment temptation hits. Write down the person (or people) who you feel God wants to use as your prayer targets the next time you are mentally battling temptation. Write down the specific things you plan to ask God on their behalf.

Colby-so smart...
Chris-wants nothing to do w/ Christ...
Dani - is questionable...

5. On page 141 of *Authentic Beauty*, I talk about the importance of "taking a different street" instead of continuing to fall into the same sin. Is there a particular sin that you struggle with over and over again in your life? If so, ask God to show you how to "take a different street" in that area. Write down the practical changes that you need to make to avoid the same pitfalls again. Be as specific as possible.

There isn't a sin I keep falling into.

OVERCOMING ROADBLOCKS

What's the big deal?

The Enemy of our souls is very clever. Once we begin allowing God to purify our lives from sin and teach us how to take temptation seriously, Satan will cause us to question whether subtle sins are really such a big deal after all. It starts with a tiny seed—a voice in the back of your mind, enticing you with dangerous little thoughts: *Look at her; she's doing it and she seems to be just fine! What's so wrong with a little flirting anyway?* Or, *My life would be so much better if I could just be in a relationship with him. Maybe he's not the perfect Christian, but I'm sure I would be a good influence on his life if we were together.* Or, *If a Christian leader I respect says it is okay, who am I to argue? The leader knows so much more than I do.* Or, *I've already messed up so many times—it's too late for me anyway, so why should I bother trying to live differently?*

If you find yourself asking the question "What's the big deal?" about any questionable thing in your life, then it's time to realign your perspective with God's. It's time to put the battle secrets we just learned into practice. Sin, no matter how seemingly small, *is* a big deal to God. It hinders us from experiencing the lives He created us to live. It creates a wall between us and Him. It squelches our thriving romance with Him.

Read **Matthew 5:29–30**, and ask God to make you willing to do whatever it takes, no matter how radical it seems, to keep sin from taking root in your heart. We must remain on guard against sin each and every day of our lives. We are either heading toward light or heading toward darkness. We can't head in both directions at the same time. As Oswald Chambers observed, "Turn away for one second from obedience, and instantly darkness and death are at work."[20]

Can I really gain victory over sin?

If you struggle with the same sins over and over again, it is tempting to believe that you will never see victory this side of heaven. Even many modern Christian voices (in the form of Christian books, Christian music, and Christian messages) tell us that being enslaved to sin is part of a normal Christian existence.

Of course, if we try to overcome the power of sin in our own strength and determination, we will fail every time. Only one power is strong enough to defeat sin—the power of God. The secret to gaining victory over sin is to allow Jesus Christ to overtake our being and to yield to His supernatural, enabling power within us.

Grace, as defined in the New Testament, is not merely the "hug" or acceptance of God. Grace is the enabling power of God to accomplish on our behalf what we are incapable of accomplishing on our own. There are about one hundred verses in the Bible that define grace in this way, but here are just a few: Romans 1:5; 1 Corinthians 3:10; 2 Corinthians 12:9; 2 Thessalonians 1:12; and 1 Peter 5:10.

Kick out the lie that you are a helpless victim who will always be enslaved to sin. You are called to live a life *victorious over sin,* a life that showcases the light of God—not through your own strength but through the strength of Christ within you, as it says in Colossians 1:27. Ian Thomas expresses it beautifully:

> It is not a matter of doing our best for Him, but of Christ being His best in us. All that He is in all that we are. We can never have more…and need never enjoy less![21]

9

Feminine Mystique
and Romance

Future Husband Application

*E*VERY STAGE of a love story that is initiated by our Prince—both the friendship and the romance—only enhances our intimacy with Him. A relationship that leads us closer to our Prince and carefully protects our inner sanctuary is the key to discovering romance as it was intended to be.

OPENING UP

1. Do you believe that God is always faithful? In what ways has God already proven Himself faithful in your life? Read **Genesis 21:1–7**, and meditate on the faithfulness of God.

   God is faithful to me with the friends He's placed in my life, my family and food.

2. Have you ever seen a woman whose heart is fully captured by Jesus Christ? What was it about her life that inspired you? *Scripture suggestion:* **1 Corinthians 7:34.**

   They attracted ppl. They're different from everyone else... draw you to them.

3. How do you feel about letting Christ meet the deepest needs of your heart, even before you find your future spouse? In what ways has your relationship with Christ already fulfilled your dreams and desires? *Scripture suggestions:* **Psalm 37:4; 73:25–26; 1 John 2:17.**

I feel excited!

I feel loved, cared for and like I can go to him for any reason. Anything

Like an apple tree among the trees of the forest,
So is my beloved among the young men.
In his shade I took great delight and sat down,
And his fruit was sweet to my taste. (Song of Solomon 2:3)

Life Meaning: When we delight in God's presence, we are refreshed, renewed, and filled with satisfaction and contentment. He is our hearts' one desire. Spending time with Him, sitting in His presence, knowing His heart will naturally place all other things in our lives—including romance and relationships—into their proper positions. Our souls will be at rest!

THE NEXT LEVEL

1. Think about what consumes the majority of your thoughts throughout the day. In what ways do your most common thoughts reflect a heart focused on Christ? In what ways do they reflect a heart focused on relationships with guys?

   75% guys
   25% God — Not OK

2. Do you crave male attention and have a need to be found attractive? How does God want you to handle this desire? *Scripture suggestions:* **Psalm 27:8; Romans 12:2.**

   Nope

3. What kind of man do you hope to win? Are your actions and attitudes appealing to worldly, self-focused, culture-trained guys? Or, like Sarah Edwards from page 75, will your lifestyle appeal to a Christ-built man of God? (Option: Write down how your actions and attitudes might need to change if you hope to win the heart of a truly Christlike guy and keep

yourself unstained by the pollution of this world.) *Scripture suggestion:*
2 Corinthians 7:1; James 1:27; 2 Peter 3:11.

Spend more time meditating on the Lord throughout the day.

Waiting for My Isaac
(BY BRIANNE, 25, WISCONSIN)

In Genesis 16, God promised a son to Abraham and Sarah in their old age.
But Sarah did not trust God to fulfill this promise. She decided to take matters into her own hands and gave her maidservant Hagar to be with Abraham
in order to produce a child for their family line. When Hagar bore Abraham's
son, he was not the child God had promised. He was named Ishmael, which
means, "He will be a wild donkey of a man; his hand will be against everyone
and everyone's hand against him, and he will live in hostility toward all his
brothers" (Genesis 16:12, NIV). God had promised Isaac—a son born to
Abraham out of Sarah's womb. But Sarah rushed ahead of God, and it only
led to heartache.

(continued on next page)

In my own life, I've created many "Ishmaels" in the area of relationships, manipulating a person or situation in an attempt to fulfill the desire for companionship that God has placed in my heart. At times my longing for an earthly romance has consumed me. God has promised me an Isaac, but I have rushed ahead of Him and tried to produce an Ishmael out of impatience.

When I first began college, I tried to stay as far away from the male of the species as possible to bypass the mistakes I had made in the past. But eventually, I befriended someone. I began to spend hours each week with this someone. He became my closest friend, a person to confide in and share life with.

The friendship seemed so right—fun loving yet focused on God. We talked about what we were learning about God and even prayed together. What on earth could be wrong with that? But in my heart of hearts I knew I had an unhealthy attachment to this relationship. I felt a constant pull on my heart by the Spirit of God. His whisperings were continuous. I knew He wanted to direct my steps and keep me safe, yet I ignored His voice, choosing my desires over His and rationalizing my way through the relationship.

Looking back now, I can see how self-focused the relationship became over time. I wanted this friendship because in it I could taste the fulfillment of my deep desire for companionship. I called it a friendship, yet I was trying in my own subtle ways to fan into flame something more. All along, I knew from my inner hesitancy that if I were truly yielded to Christ, I wouldn't be going so far to hold on to something that was never supposed to be there.

Through much prayer, God showed me that this friendship was not drawing me more deeply into His presence. He softly reminded me that only intimacy with Him could truly fulfill me. By His grace He plucked the beginnings of an Ishmael right out of my heart, and by His strong but loving hand of discipline upon me, I ended the friendship.

Believe me, walking in obedience to God is not always an easy thing. In this case it was extremely difficult. But God gave me the strength to let the friendship go and to trust Him to bring my Isaac in His own perfect time and way.

I am still waiting for my Isaac. But now I am content. There is not a safer, more blessed place to be in this world than at the center of God's will, trusting Him with all things. I know that when God fulfilled His promise by giving Abraham and Sarah a son named Isaac, he brought laughter and joy—and Abraham and Sarah marveled at God's supernatural work in their lives.

If you hear that still, small voice whispering to you, draw near to listen. Let God direct you into the amazing plans He has for you. Awaiting you is a life filled with "Isaacs"—blessings poured out by the Spirit of God into your life, if only you will choose to wait for Him to fulfill what He has in store for you.

FOR PERSONAL REFLECTION, PRAYER, AND STUDY

1. Write down some specific traits that mark a God-built love story. If you are in a relationship, compare your current reality with your list. Does your relationship motivate you to become more and more like Christ? Or does it cause you to focus on yourself and your own desires? If you are in a relationship that you know is not honoring to Christ, *now is the time to let that relationship go.* No matter how hard it may be, you will never go wrong in exchanging your own agenda for God's very best.

2. Guarding feminine mystique cannot merely be a good idea that we agree with; it must pervade every aspect of our lives. Remember that we are not called to be thorns with a hint of lily whiteness. We are called to be lilies among thorns, to live a truly set-apart existence in the midst of a perverse generation. Prayerfully answer the following questions (also found on page 161 of *Authentic Beauty*), and allow God to change your heart and attitude wherever needed.

   • *Have I allowed the culture to convince me that my feminine mystique is worthless?* Read **Psalm 45:10–15; Proverbs 31:10–12;** and **Song**

of Solomon 2:7. Write down what God is speaking to your heart about guarding your mystique.

- *Have I given away pieces of my heart, mind, emotions, or body, or even performed sexual favors to receive the approval of guys?* Repent where repentance is needed, and allow God to cleanse you of sin you have allowed into your life in this area. Read **1 Timothy 4:12; 5:1–2;** and **Ephesians 5:3** about God's desire for our conduct with the opposite sex. Write down what God is speaking to your heart about protecting your heart and body from this day forward.

- *Have I adopted the careless attitude of today's young women—encouraging the sexual attention of guys around me by the way I act or dress?* Read **1 Timothy 2:8–10** and **Proverbs** 7 and write down what God is speaking to your heart about how you should dress and act around the opposite sex.

  To dress modestly, decent, apropriate, good deeds and to worship

- *Have I settled for less than a Christlike guy because I don't truly believe my Prince can bring anyone better into my life in His perfect time and way?* Read **1 Samuel 2:30; Psalm 27:14; 84:11; 130:5–6.** Write down what God is speaking to your heart about the reward of waiting for His very best.

  NOPE

  Happiness, peace

3. Are there any influences that are pulling you away from guarding your feminine mystique? Be aware that certain "Christian" influences in our lives might need to be questioned and even eliminated (see page 164 of *Authentic Beauty*). Read **2 Timothy 3:2–5** and **Hebrews 12:1–2.** List any specific hindrances (whether they be people, activities, or influences) that you feel God is calling you to eliminate from your life.

friends, TV

OVERCOMING ROADBLOCKS

How can I really love my future husband right now?

Before you actually meet the man you are going to marry, it is easy to think of him as an ethereal concept rather than a real, live person walking around on this earth. But your future husband isn't just a concept—he is a real person with real feelings. In order to truly love him, begin living as if he could see your actions and attitudes toward the opposite sex. If he were watching you interact with guys, would he feel honored? Or would he feel hurt and jealous? You may not be able to talk to him, but you can physically, mentally, and emotionally *love him right now* by setting your life aside for him. If you give him this amazing gift, you will strengthen the foundation of your love story in ways you can't even imagine, because you will be building your romance upon the sacrificial, selfless love of Jesus Christ.

Here are some practical ways you can begin loving your future spouse today:

- Make a prayer list for your husband. Pray every day for him to remain pure and to be a godly man, to be shaped into the Warrior Poet likeness of Christ.
- Write him love letters when you are lonely. Tell him you are waiting for him and describe your commitment to remain set apart for him alone.
- Memorize scriptures about purity and set-apartness and meditate on them often. (Some examples: **Proverbs 31:12; 1 Timothy 4:12; 2 Timothy 2:22.**)
- Choose verses to pray for your husband, such as Psalm 37:31: "The law of his God is in his heart; none of his steps shall slide" (KJV).
- Make a no-compromise list. What are your specific commitments for your future husband? And what, specifically, are you waiting for in a man? A list can remind you not to settle for less than God's best.

The Making of Warriors

1. Why are modern guys confused when it comes to relating to women? Think about the guys in your own life. How can you begin leading them closer to Christ through your life and actions?

2. Why does a woman have such influence in a man's life? How can you begin to use your feminine power for good and not harm? Ask God to show you any ways in which you have been manipulative toward guys. Write down the practical actions you can take in order to begin shaping guys into Christ-built warriors rather than trying to control or manipulate them for your own agenda.

tender
reverence

the passion
of a set-apart
young woman

His whispers are sweetness itself,
wholly desirable.

SONG OF SONGS 5:16, NEB

Cultivating Intimacy

Going Deeper with Your Prince

DAILY, PASSIONATE intimacy with our Prince does not automatically happen; it must be nurtured in order to grow. As A. W. Tozer said, "The one who would know God must give time to Him."[22]

OPENING UP

1. Where does true worship flow from? Do you feel you have an attitude of tender reverence toward Christ? What are some ways you can cultivate a heart of true worship? (Option: Choose two or three psalms to read through. As you read, ask Christ to awaken you to the reality of who He is.) *Scripture suggestions:* **Job 1:19–21; Psalm 29:1–2.**

2. Worship is a lifestyle. If we are not worshiping Him with our lives, then we are worshiping something else—such as self, money, or success. What does it mean to worship Christ with your life? *Scripture suggestions:* **John 4:24; Romans 12:1.**

   To lean on. Depend on.

3. It is easy to justify away the need to spend time cultivating our intimacy with Christ when we are so busy trying to solve our problems on our own. What problems is He asking you to trust Him with? *Scripture suggestion:* **Jeremiah 10:23.**

Life in general.

An Appointment with the King

(EXCERPT FROM
WHEN GOD WRITES YOUR LIFE STORY)

As the story goes, a traveling evangelist in England in the eighteenth century was asked to appear before one of the most prestigious and influential men in the country. Many had sought an audience with this rich lord, but only a few were granted the illustrious privilege of his company for an evening.

The evangelist welcomed the opportunity to share a meal with

(continued on next page)

this man who was interested in understanding more about his work for Christ throughout the English countryside. But as the night waxed on and the clock struck seven, the evangelist rose from the table and declared plainly, "Thank you for a wonderful evening, but I must be going."

Startled by this man's impertinence and disregard for English custom, the rich lord replied, "Do you not know that my table is the most highly sought-after table in England? I receive hundreds of requests each day to gain my audience. Do you have the audacity to remove yourself before our night is through?"

The humble evangelist looked back toward the rich lord with a confidence in his eyes that was shocking to the wealthy kinglet. And in a very certain tone he said, "I have an appointment with the Lord of heaven and earth, and I dare not be tired and I dare not be late."

How many of us today possess that kind of spiritual discipline? How many of us have that kind of unswerving, unfaltering commitment to God? How many of us are so devoted to Him that we count time spent in His presence more valuable than any other opportunity that comes our way? If knowing God is our true purpose, then we must make our relationship with Him our highest priority. Not just in theory, but in every moment of the day.

Brother Lawrence, a gentle monk who lived in the 1600s, called it "practicing the presence of God." Lawrence made it his utmost endeavor to live with a continual sense of God's presence and to never forget about Him, even for a moment. He worked as a cook in the monastery's kitchen, and as he began his tasks each morning, he dedicated his day to his Creator. As he went about his tasks, he conversed in familiar conversation with his Maker, imploring God's grace and offering every action as a sacrifice to Him.

"There is not in the world a kind of love more sweet and delightful than that of a continual conversation with God," wrote Lawrence. "Those only can comprehend it who practice and experience it."

God is far less concerned about what we do for Him than He is about our passion to simply be with Him. He isn't impressed with numbers or achievements like we are. He is moved by the daily act of surrender. He is stirred by our desire to know Him more.

Choosing the right college, career, ministry, and spouse is important. But most of us become so caught up in making those key decisions that we fail to build on the foundation stone of a successful life—bringing our entire existence under the control of God Almighty every hour of the day. Two thousand years ago Jesus told His disciples, "First, seek My loving control over your life, My kingdom-rule over your soul, and then I will be sure to take care of all the other details of your life" (see Matthew 6:33).[23]

THE NEXT LEVEL

1. Do you think of knowing Christ as an endless frontier of possibility and discovery? Or have you become complacent, feeling like your relationship with Him has gone as deep as it will ever go? How do you think God wants to expand your vision for seeking more and more of Him? *Scripture suggestions:* **Psalm 139:1–12; Ephesians 3:18.**

   I am deep with Christ but want to keep going for as long as I live.

2. Helen Keller said, "Life is either a daring adventure or nothing."[24] How does God want you to live? Which areas of your life need to be transformed from a dull drudgery into an exciting adventure with Christ? *Scripture suggestions:* **John 10:10; Hebrews 11:32–35.**

FOR PERSONAL REFLECTION, PRAYER, AND STUDY

1. Three of the most critical elements for nurturing intimacy with Christ are *order, calm,* and *sanctuary.* Read the descriptions of these elements below, and ask God to show how you might need to change your life or environment in order to make each one a reality in your daily existence.

   Order: Having an ordered life takes effort, but it creates the security of knowing that the important things are being preserved and emphasized daily. Do you have a chaotic schedule that causes you to waste hours on meaningless activities? Is your home environment so messy that you can't find your Bible? Let God's Spirit gently reveal the things in your life that need some focus, and then begin to tackle them one step at a time. Read **Colossians 3:15.**

   > Take off your sandals, for the place where you are standing is holy ground. (Exodus 3:5, NIV)

   Calm: Everything about the world we live in is chaotic and fast paced, but everything about God is peaceful and patient. To cultivate His presence, you must create an atmosphere that resembles His presence. Ask God to reveal to you which areas of your life need to be transformed by His supernatural calm. Do you need to change the way you react to stress? learn to trust Him when bad news hits? slow down your overall pace of life in order to more clearly hear His whisper? Read **Isaiah 26:3** and **James 3:18.**

   Sanctuary: Even though you may be used to being surrounded by people, a healthy life demands a degree of aloneness. You need a sanctuary in your life that you can escape to—a quiet place where you can think,

PRACTICAL STEPS FOR GOING DEEPER WITH CHRIST

Here are some specific ways to cultivate your relationship with Christ. As you read this list, add other things the Lord shows you. Pray that you may be in tune to His voice, aligned with His will, and obedient to His call. Remember, "draw near to God and He will draw near to you" (James 4:8, NKJV). He will open your eyes to all the perfect ways intimacy with Him can be nurtured in your unique life.

- Read and meditate on the Bible (start with Psalms and Proverbs or Matthew, Mark, Luke, or John).
- Study specific biblical characters (such as Esther, Ruth, David, and Stephen).
- Use a concordance to learn the true meaning of words in the Bible.
- Study online resources, such as www.precept.org, www.biblegateway.org, www.authenticgirl.com, and www.whengodwrites.com.
- Sing worship music.
- Pray with an accountability partner.
- Go on dates with Jesus—even talk to Him on your cell phone in public!
- Do devotions outside in God's creation.
- Journal prayer requests, answered prayer, and meditations on truth.

• Read Christian literature about godly men and women. The
following books have had a huge impact on my life:

A Chance to Die: The Life and Legacy of Amy Carmichael
by Elisabeth Elliot

The Cross and the Switchblade
by David Wilkerson

Foxes' Book of Martyrs by John Foxe

Gladys Aylward: The Little Woman
by Gladys Aylward with Christine Hunter

Gold Cord by Amy Carmichael

Great Women of the Christian Faith
by Edith Deen (look for a used copy online)

Hearts of Fire by Voice of the Martyrs

The Hiding Place by Corrie ten Boom

Hudson Taylor's Spiritual Secret
by Dr. and Mrs. Howard Taylor

If I Perish by Esther Ahn Kim

Oswald Chambers: Abandoned to God
by David McCasland

Shadow of the Almighty by Elisabeth Elliot

Tortured for Christ
by Richard Wurmbrand

meditate, study, pray, and be still. Whether you find your place of retreat outside near the big oak tree or in the farthest corner of your bedroom closet, do whatever you must do to find a way to bring an element of privacy to every day of your life. Read **Mark 1:35.** Spend some time thinking about where and how you can create a solitary place for your daily times with Christ. Write down any specific steps you must take to create that environment.

Find a time in the day when I don't have to worry about anything but God.

2. A married couple cannot build a lifetime of intimacy in a one-week honeymoon, and neither can we build a lifetime of intimacy with Christ on the high of a one-time spiritual retreat. Read **Jeremiah 29:13.** Are you seeking Christ with your whole heart, or are you only experiencing periodic, mountaintop experiences with Him? Ask Him to show you practical ways in which you can pursue Him daily, not just a few times a year at spiritual events.

3. A beautiful picture of what it means to put Christ above all else can be found in **Luke 10:38–42.** As you read this story, think about your own life. Are you like Martha, so consumed by stress, anxiety, and busyness that you have no time to sit at Christ's feet? What things in your life do you sometimes give higher importance to than spending time with Christ? In what ways might God want to make you more like Mary?

Not to stress over school / friends

4. Nothing strengthens intimacy with Christ more than a sense of His finger-prints on our lives. As you have worked your way through *Authentic Beauty,* how has your perspective on your relationship with Christ changed? Reflect back to your life a few weeks ago. How specifically has God been working in your life?

I feel like I want to learn and spend time with him. I always have but the feeling of it is stronger and almost more exciting.

He IS Love

(BY ASHLEY, 22, WASHINGTON)

Seek first His kingdom and His righteousness, and all these things will be added to you. (Matthew 6:33)

At the beginning of the second semester of my senior year in college, the buzz on campus revolved solely around postcollege plans. As friends of mine started to have jobs open up or wedding rings adorn their fingers, I couldn't help but wonder if the Lord had anything for me.

During that time of questioning the Lord's provision and faithfulness, He spoke something to my heart that has radically changed how I view His love. *"Ashley, anytime you are jealous or envious of another person's life, it is when you are not trusting Me and what I have for you."* That revelation was so necessary and timely. Without even realizing it, I had begun to believe that the Lord must love my friends more than He loved me, because He had opened doors and presented opportunities for them to pursue while I felt forgotten. Here I was, about to graduate, and I thought the Lord must not love me as much because my life didn't look as good, abundant, or fruitful as those around me. He reminded me, once again, that His love for me does not change.

It is so easy to measure the power, perfection, or reality of God's love based on our personal circumstances. We think, *He must love me a lot right now, because everything in my life is great.* Or, *He must be mad at me because nothing seems to be going right.* The truth is that He IS, and He never changes. He is always perfect, always love, always just, always powerful, and always faithful to who He is. Our ideas of what is perfect, loving, and fair might not always match His, but His love for us never decreases and never increases. It is always perfect and complete.

When we think the Lord is mean, unfair, unfaithful and untrustworthy, is it because He *is* those things? Or is it because we are focusing too much on our lives rather than His?

The Lord wants us to want *Him*. He doesn't want our primary focus to be on what He does for us. He wants our eyes set on His life, His kingdom, His salvation, and His love. He alone fulfills.

The world might look at my life and wonder why I would continue to serve Him even when things are difficult. But I just smile and remember that the circumstances in my life do not define the Lord's love… He IS love.

5. Andrew Murray said, "With the deepest feeling of my soul I can say that I am satisfied with Jesus now; but there is also the consciousness of how much fuller the revelation can be of the exceeding abundance of His grace. Let us never hesitate to say, *this is only the beginning.*"[25] How would you like to know Christ more this year? Do you desire to grasp a greater depth of His love? a clearer picture of His glory and majesty? an awareness of His presence throughout the day? the ability to communicate with Him continuously? Write down your desires and ask Him to fulfill them in His own perfect way.

lord, I want all of you, always will, forever and always. I want to be apart of you and you of me every day of my life. I want people to see the difference and ask. lord, that can only happen with/through you. Please do that for me. make me stronger in you every day of my life.
- amen

OVERCOMING ROADBLOCKS

Why does my relationship with Christ grow stale?

It is all too easy to try to grow our relationship with Christ through our own self-efforts. Self-propagated spirituality is what leads to a stale relationship with Christ; we strive and strain to grow closer to Him, but we become spiritually stagnant the moment that life takes a stressful or hectic turn. Only His supernatural, enabling power can equip us to pursue Him and build our lives around Him through all the ups and downs of life. Prayerfully think through your answers to the following questions:

- Are you dictating your life's agenda and begging God's blessing on your decisions? If so, you are on the road to producing an Ishmael version, rather than an Isaac version, of Christianity.

- Are you determining your own daily schedule without inviting God to incorporate His hourly agenda? True Christianity involves Christ's possessing our very existence, His operating our lives according to His plan, and our merely yielding to His sovereign will.

- When you read the Bible, do you try to imitate Christ out of human effort? If so, then your heart may be right, but your spiritual fruit will be moldy.

- Are you anticipating God's direction in your life and then taking the pen back and finishing the chapter? While your heart's desire is to accomplish God's agenda in your life, has self once again taken the helm?

Fully yielding to God's manner, His method, and His timing brings about a heavenly result for which no human can possibly receive credit. Read **Psalm 46:10.** We must be still and know that He is God and trust that He alone is capable of performing all that He has promised to perform. Rather than striving and straining to find Him, we must realize that He is right beside us, asking us to yield to His loving control.

11

Confident Sparkle

The Unwavering Strength of the Set-Apart Life

CHRIST ASKS US to deny ourselves, take up our cross, and follow Him (see Matthew 16:24). The secret to gaining the confident sparkle of Christ is to get rid of self-focus and instead become entirely consumed with knowing and serving Jesus Christ.

OPENING UP

1. Have you ever observed someone whose radiance and selflessness makes her shine in the midst of darkness? What should our lives look like in contrast to this world? *Scripture suggestions:* **Matthew 5:16; Philippians 2:15.**

   amongst everyone who is not a born again Christian, we must be different from them in a way that is mystrious to them. They can see God shown in us, through our actions.

2. We can only radiate God's glory when we become consumed with Him alone. As Bishop John W. Bardsley writes, "Caring not at all what the world thinks of you, because you are entirely taken up with the reality of God."[26] In what areas of your life do you need to become less self-conscious and more Christ-conscious? *Scripture suggestions:* **Psalm 56:11; 118:8–9.**

   I need to become less self conscious with the music I listen to. People laugh and ask - sometimes I get embarassed when I know there's no reason to.

3. Do you gain your ⟨confidence⟩ from your <u>popularity</u>, a <u>relationship</u>, <u>the</u> <u>attention of guys</u>, <u>your talents</u>, or your <u>appearance</u>? Why is it dangerous to our spiritual lives to look outside of Christ for security, confidence, and approval? *Scripture suggestion:* **1 Thessalonians 2:4.**

It is not what God wants or intended. It's like saying God is not enough and that's not alright. We need to have complete confidence and approval in God and God alone.

This week, determine not to base your contentment on your circumstances. Don't attach your happiness to what others think of you. Remain rooted in the unchanging, unwavering, unfaltering love of your true Prince, and <u>you</u> <u>will glow</u> from the inside out. As Oswald Chambers said, "We have to battle through our moods into absolute devotion to the Lord Jesus. <u>We must set</u> <u>aside preoccupation with our circumstances and experiences, and learn aban-</u> <u>doned devotion to Him.</u>"[27]

THE NEXT LEVEL

1. The entire reason for creating and protecting the sacred sanctuary within your heart is for the purpose of *enjoying* passionate, tender intimacy with your Prince every day of your life. In what practical ways can you begin to walk with His Spirit, aware of His presence and communicating with Him throughout your day? *Scripture suggestions:* **Psalm 61:2; Isaiah 58:11; John 16:13; Galatians 5:25.** (Suggested reading: *Abide in Christ* by Andrew Murray and *The Practice of the Presence of God* by Brother Lawrence.)

   Thust him and let him be the leader of my life.

2. Amy Carmichael wrote, "All too many Christians break down, not because of their circumstances, but because of a weary, fretting spirit too rushed to dwell in peace."[28] Read **Psalm 16:11; 46:10;** and **Isaiah 32:17.** What habits, distractions, or activities in your life might need to be shifted, removed, or altered for you to have a quieter mind?

   Some T.V. time, texting.

Yielding to His Strength

(BY ANNIE, 21, IDAHO)

I called on the LORD in distress;
The LORD answered me and set me in a broad place.
The LORD is on my side;
I will not fear. (Psalm 118:5–6, NKJV)

Three years ago I found myself standing at the entrance of an old building that sat within the boundaries of a small leprosy rehab village in southern China. I was there with a team on a short missions trip, and our visit to this village had been a last-minute addition to our schedule.

As we entered the abandoned building, my team moved to the right, but glancing to the left, I saw that Buddy, our interpreter, had knelt down in a small space that appeared to be someone's miserable home. As my group pulled farther away, something gripped my heart and pulled me into the small space that held an untold story.

From his position on the floor, Buddy spoke out to me, "Annie, come here." I got down on my hands and knees and scooted in beside him. Buddy was holding the hand of a leper woman, who sat cross-legged upon a few boards. Everything about her appearance jarred my senses. She sat among many worn, smelly rags and crates of belongings while bugs crawled over her. On her hands where fingers should have been, only scarred stubs remained.

(continued on next page)

Her feet, twisted beneath her, were bound with rags and appeared to be half the size of even a petite woman's feet. Her eyes were red, sunken in, and glazed over, now blind from the effects of the nerve damage that leprosy had caused. Her skin was covered in wounds, dry and calloused; her hair short and gray. Buddy told me that she was in her fifties, but she looked like someone well into her seventies. My eyes drifted back to her dirty, crippled hands. They were reached out and clinging to the whole, clean hands of Buddy beside me.

As I took this in, Buddy turned to me and said, "Here, Annie, take her hands."

Everything in me shouted, *No! I can't!* But I slowly nodded my head. He pulled her hands over and placed them within mine. They felt rough and foreign the moment our skin touched. She began rubbing them back and forth so abruptly that I wanted to pull away.

"It's okay, Annie. She's lost the feeling in her hands and is just trying to feel your touch," said Buddy.

I cringed at my lack of compassion. I wanted so badly to do something, but I was repulsed by everything that surrounded me.

Putting my head down in discomfort, I pleaded with the Lord, *Show me what to do, Jesus. I know that You love this woman and have put her hands within mine. Show me how to love her. I can't do this on my own, Father. Nothing in me can do this.*

When I looked up, there sat before me the most beautiful sight. The precious woman before me was still scarred and deformed. She was dirty and infected. She was rejected and unlovely. She was still a leper. Yet, now when I looked at her, I felt the eyes of my Jesus looking through me onto her deformed and ragged body. I saw a woman so loved by Him. To Him she was flawless, she was whole, and she was in need.

A new peace enlarged within me, and unhindered love began to spill out. I removed my hands from hers and put them around her back in an embrace. Her body began to tremble, and tears spilled out from her blinded eyes. She began speaking a phrase in Chinese over and over until I asked Buddy what she was saying.

Her words were simple: "I've missed you, I've missed you, I've missed you."

In that brief encounter, I learned the power of God's love and life within the heart of a yielded Christian. I sat at this woman's feet in total helplessness, yet I experienced the treasure of God's sufficiency. I learned that no matter how difficult the circumstances surrounding me or how inadequate I am for what God calls me to, His grace is sufficient for each challenge in my life.

I'll never forget the words of that dear woman, blind and abandoned: "I've missed you." I knew she did not mean me. Two months earlier another group of believers had visited and ministered to her. They too had loved her from the well of God's rich love. I have never had a clearer picture of the power of Christ's life. She could not see me, but she did see a perfect love beyond my own capacity that reached out to embrace her. When I was brought to the end of my striving, when I accepted that I couldn't do anything in my own power—that was the key to discovering what *His* life in me is capable of when my soul is yielded to Him.

3. What do you think about as you are drifting off to sleep at night? How might God want to change your nightly meditations? What are some practical ways you can begin to shift your nighttime thoughts (such as through prayer, reading Scripture, listening to worship music as you fall asleep, or meditating on truth)? *Scripture suggestions:* **Psalm 63:6; Philippians 4:8.**

   I already do all of those...

FOR PERSONAL REFLECTION, PRAYER, AND STUDY

1. During times of worship, does your mind wander distractedly? Do you have a true heart of worship for your Prince that lasts throughout the day? What are some ways that you can cultivate true, heartfelt worship for Christ in your life? (Ideas: Spend time outdoors in His beautiful creation, journaling what you observe about His nature; plan times alone to listen to worship music and meditate on Him; read through the psalms and gain a clear picture of His glory.) Write down some specific ways you feel God wants you to cultivate a lifestyle of worship.

2. How do you currently interact with Scripture? Biblical meditation involves actively pondering and processing truth until it becomes an integral part of who you are. Read **Joshua 1:8** and **Psalm 1:2**. Write down some practical steps you can take to begin allowing God to speak to your heart and mind with practical applications of His Word. (Ideas: Get study tools to assist you in gaining a deeper understanding of the verses you read; listen to Bible-on-CD recordings as you drive in your car or lie in bed at night; do an inductive Bible study, such as those found on www.precept.org.)

Who is this coming up from the wilderness,
Leaning upon her beloved? (Song of Solomon 8:5, NKJV)

Life Meaning: To radiate with unshakable peace and confidence in this life, we must not look to ourselves. Rather, we must lean wholly and completely upon the strong arm of our beloved Prince and allow Him to fill us with His strength, His confidence, and His unshakable calm in the midst of life's storms.

3. While Christian books can certainly enhance our relationship with Christ, they should never take the place of personal, diligent study of the Word of God. This is especially true today, since many modern books subtly twist or dilute the message of Scripture. The more we acquaint ourselves with God's Word, the quicker we will recognize dangerous messages that undermine our understanding of who Christ really is. Read **1 Timothy 4:16.** Take a few moments to write down a general game plan for your times of study, with an emphasis on studying God's Word. (For example, you could allot thirty minutes to studying Scripture, twenty minutes to journaling and prayer, and ten or fifteen minutes to reading a Christian book or devotional.) List specific books, chapters, or characters in the Bible you want to study in depth and what tools you will need to do so.

4. Which aspect of Betsy ten Boom's story (pages 207–12 in *Authentic Beauty*) impacts you most? Are you willing to accept the call of Christ to love with His love, even when it seems humanly impossible? Write down your heart's response to His call upon your life.

OVERCOMING ROADBLOCKS

What about ME? *What's so wrong with building my Christian walk around my own emotions, feelings, or uniqueness?*

Ian Thomas wrote, "The Christian life can be explained only in terms of Jesus Christ, and if your life as a Christian can still be explained in terms of you—your personality, your willpower, your gift, your talent, your money, your courage, your scholarship, your dedication, your sacrifice, or your anything—then although you may have the Christian life, you are not yet living it."[29]

> If the praise of others elates me, and the criticism of others depresses me, then I am not truly resting in my Prince's love.
>
> AMY CARMICHAEL[30]

In modern Christianity, we have become consumed with examining our own emotions, wounds, and desires. It is true that God cares about our feelings, hurts, hopes, and fears, but He does not want our emotions to be the focal point of our interaction with Him.

If Betsy ten Boom had focused on her own emotions and hurts during her time of imprisonment, she would have crumbled under the weight of her suffering. Instead, she focused on the amazing love of Jesus Christ and received His supernatural, enabling grace that allowed her to walk through those trials triumphantly. When Stephen was being stoned for his faith in Acts 7:55–60, he did not turn inward and focus on his own hurt, fear, or pain. Rather, he turned his eyes to heaven and saw the glory of God and Jesus Christ standing at the right hand of the Father.

The Bible exhorts us toward self-denial—not self-focus, self-pity, or self-glory. In fact, an accurate definition of *sin* would be "self on the throne of one's life." That is why we must put self in its proper place: a submissive servant to the life of Jesus Christ within us.

It is very true that God animates and indwells each of our unique personalities. Yet we must keep in mind that He does this not to showcase us but to showcase Himself. As we become set apart for Him, He transforms us with His own amazing beauty, but we should never stand in the way of His being seen for who He really is.

God desires to work through our uniqueness and talents. When Christ is our focal point, we become everything we are meant to be—a servant to the glory of the King of all kings.

A. W. Tozer said it well:

> Deliverance can come to us only by the defeat of our old life (self on the throne). Safety and peace come only after we have been forced to our knees. God rescues us by breaking us, by shattering our strength and wiping out our resistance. Then He invades our natures with that ancient and eternal life which is from the beginning. So He conquers us and by that benign conquest, saves us for Himself.[32]

It is a tremendous emancipation to get rid of every kind of self-consideration and learn to heed only one thing—the relationship between Christ and ourselves.

OSWALD CHAMBERS[31]

12

Preparing for Intimacy

Future Husband Application

*T*RUE INTIMACY is sharing life with someone at the deepest level—knowing someone completely and being known completely in return. True human intimacy can be built upon only one foundation: the love of our Prince, Jesus Christ. Physical, mental, and emotional bonds only grow more amazing when we build upon this unshakable foundation of Christ's heroic, sacrificial, and unconditional love.

OPENING UP

1. What does healthy, Christ-built intimacy look like in a marriage? How can you prepare now for true intimacy with your spouse someday?

    They both grow stronger in God b/c of eachother. Praying... I will find true love with the lord.

2. How can you keep your intimacy with Christ at the center of your existence, even in an earthly relationship and marriage? How can you avoid looking to an earthly spouse to fill needs in your heart that only Christ can meet? *Scripture suggestion:* **Isaiah 58:11.**

    Base your relationship on the Lord & your feelings. Build a strong relationship with the Lord before anything else. Stay in the word.

3. Why is it important for spiritual unity to be the foundation of a friend-ship or relationship? Have you ever built a relationship upon emotion or physical attraction? What was the result?

Yes, it was horrible. Hearts were broken and the realization that nothing was ever there. The lord is the guidance of us and is the reason for everything... sets a reason anyway.

THE NEXT LEVEL

1. What are the advantages of savoring a season of friendship before a rela-tionship begins? How do you desire to build a relationship with your future husband? In what ways do you plan to keep Christ at the fore-front?

You get to know eachother, really understand eachother I want to hang out, laugh with the fam(s), adventure. The Lord will already have that special relationship w/ me.

Keeping an Open Hand

(EXCERPT FROM *TEACHING TRUE LOVE TO A SEX-AT-13 GENERATION*)

On a chilly winter day in 1947, a young college girl named Elisabeth sat in the school auditorium listening to a passionate speaker. "Do not stir up or awaken love," the speaker exhorted his audience, "until God initiates the relationship." Elisabeth's heart was pricked by the challenging words. Many of her college friends had already found serious relationships. Some were engaged or married. Elisabeth felt called to a life of service for God, but she couldn't seem to ignore the longing in her heart for an earthly love story.

God was asking Elisabeth to surrender that desire to Him; to give Him the pen of her life and allow Him to script her story…even if it meant a life of singleness. Could she trust Him that much?

"God was sifting me," Elisabeth wrote later. "What kind of a God is it who asks everything of us? The same God who did not spare his own Son, but gave Him up for us all. He gives all. He asks all."

Elisabeth gave all to Him. She surrendered her longing for marriage. "I wanted to be loved," Elisabeth said. "But I [also] wanted something deeper." The "something deeper" she wanted was a Christ-ruled, Christ-centered existence. And He was asking for total control. *Lord,* she prayed, *here's my heart.*

Living out her commitment became even more challenging when she met a fiery young Christian named Jim Elliot. The more she got to know Jim, the more she saw he was the picture of everything she hoped for in a husband. "He was a real man," she said, "strong, friendly, and handsome. He loved God. That was the supreme dynamic of his life. Nothing else mattered much in comparison."

Soon Jim began to show an interest in her. But God continued to challenge her to surrender the friendship back to Him—not to cling to the hope of a relationship but to leave the pen in His hands. Elisabeth struggled deeply with the challenge. "A settled commitment to the Lord Christ and a longed-for commitment to Jim Elliot seemed to be in conflict," she wrote. "I was only a college girl, trying to do well in my studies, praying for direction for my life, attracted to a very appealing man whose primary interest was the Kingdom of God. [What was] wrong with that?"

But God wanted everything, even the "good" desires of her heart!

One day Jim told Elisabeth that he was in love with her. The revelation was bittersweet. Elisabeth's heart soared at Jim's words, but became sober again when he went on to say that God had challenged him to embrace a life of singleness—perhaps for life, or perhaps only for a season.

"I've given you and all my feelings for you to God," Jim said. "He'll have to work out whatever He wants. If I marry, I know who it will be. I want you. But you're not mine." Jim spoke of the story of Abraham's offering up of the most precious thing in his life: his son Isaac. "So I put you on the altar," he told her.

Elisabeth and Jim agreed to pray steadily about their future and wait patiently until God made the way plain. Waiting was excruciatingly difficult. *Is God interested in the plight of two college kids?* Elisabeth wondered. *Has our cause perhaps escaped His notice? Will He bother with us, when He is busy with who knows how many things?*

Elisabeth and Jim believed God wanted to be involved in the intimate details of their lives and decisions. So they continued to trust. They continued to wait. No matter how strong their feelings were, they would not rush ahead of Him.

"A good and perfect gift, these natural desires," wrote Elisabeth later. "But so much more the necessity that they be restrained, controlled, even crucified, that they might be reborn in power and purity for God. For us, this was the way we had to walk, and we walked it. Jim seeing it his duty to protect me, I seeing it mine to wait quietly, not to attempt to woo or entice."

Elisabeth and Jim didn't just wait on God for a week. They didn't just wait a month. They didn't just wait for a year. Five years passed while the two young people sought God's direction. They remained committed to each other, but they were careful to guard their emotions and pursue nothing more than a Christ-centered friendship until God showed them otherwise. The road was narrow and lonely. But Elisabeth and Jim understood the difference between self-focused human love and a love scripted by the God of creation. "A man's love for a woman ought to hold her to the highest," Elisabeth said. "Her love for him ought to do the same. I did not want to turn Jim aside from the call of God, to distract his energies, or in any way to stand between him and surrender. This was what I understood real love to mean. Purity comes at a high price. Sometimes the sacrifice makes little sense to others, but when offered to God it is always accepted."

Finally, after years of hoping, trusting, waiting, and leaving the pen in God's faithful hands, the Author of romance scripted a new chapter in their love story. He made their future clear. They felt His gentle hand guiding them to serve Him together to reach the unsaved people of South America. They were married in a simple ceremony in Ecuador in 1953.

Was the sacrifice worth it? For all their waiting and radical decisions, did Elisabeth and Jim receive anything better in the end?

"I thank my God," Jim wrote shortly before their marriage. "I was recounting today how full He has made life for me…to know that we are wholly and for always committed to one another, sold out of ourselves each for the other's good. The absolute goodness and rightness of it is unspeakable. How shall I say what I feel in gratitude to God?"

Elisabeth and Jim's love became a spectacular display of God's faithfulness and sovereignty. The decisions they made in their relationship prepared them for the adventure God called them to in their life together. They had learned sacrifice, self-giving, and implicit trust in the Creator. And soon these qualities would be put to an even greater test.

On January 8, 1956, Jim Elliot and six other missionaries were killed by Auca Indians—men whom Jim had diligently prayed for and sought to serve for six years. He willingly gave his life for the sake of Christ, and his example infused millions with passion for the gospel.

Elisabeth willingly surrendered her husband to Christ, just as she had done as a college girl in the auditorium that day. His faithful hand had scripted her story, and she knew that even in the midst of intense pain and heartache, His purpose was for her highest good.

After Jim's death, Elisabeth chose to give her life in service to the very people who had killed her husband, exemplifying the principle that she and Jim had built their marriage and life upon… "He is no fool who gives what he cannot keep to gain what he cannot lose."[33]

2. Whenever we start to cling too tightly to a friendship, relationship, or even the desire for a relationship, we must take a step back and examine our hearts. Are you allowing Christ to script out every detail of your relationship or your approach to relationships? What practical ways can you be constantly aware of the One who is writing your story?

FOR PERSONAL REFLECTION, PRAYER, AND STUDY

1. Has your heart ever been broken through a relationship? Have you allowed Christ to fully heal and restore you? If not, how does that unhealed scar affect your life today?

2. If you are dealing with unresolved pain from a broken relationship, take some time to prayerfully think through the following questions (also found on page 222 of *Authentic Beauty*). After reading the suggested scriptures, write down what God is speaking to your heart.

- Did I ever cling too tightly to the relationship for security or affirmation? Read **Psalm 16:5**.
- Did I ever put the relationship before Jesus Christ? Read **Exodus 20:3**.
- Did I ever rush ahead of God in making relational decisions? Read **Proverbs 3:5–6**.
- Did I allow my emotions to lead the way rather than allowing the tender whisper of my heavenly Prince to guide me? Read **Romans 8:1**.
- Did I ever give myself physically, mentally, or emotionally to the relationship in a way that did not reflect the lily-white likeness of my Prince? Read **1 Peter 1:16**.
- Did I knowingly entice the other person to compromise? Read **1 Corinthians 8:12**.
- Did I lash out in retaliation, verbally or otherwise, when the other person caused me pain? Read **Matthew 5:44**.
- Do I harbor bitterness or unforgiveness in my heart toward the other person? Read **Matthew 18:21–22**.

3. Have you doubted Christ's ability and desire to completely heal, restore, and set you free from a broken heart? Read **Psalm 34:18; 147:3;** and **Ezekiel 36:26.** In your own words, ask Christ to take your broken heart and begin the healing process.

4. In what ways have you allowed the words or actions of others to shape your perception of yourself rather than resting in Christ's love and desire for you? No matter what anyone on this earth says or does to you, the King of the universe, the Creator of all things, the Ruler of the heavens and earth has said that *you* are valuable. Begin filling your mind with truth, combating any lies that have been rooted in your heart. Read **Psalm 139:14–18.** Ask Christ to show you how He sees you.

5. Godly teammates are an incredible gift from God to offer hope, encouragement, and a healthy dose of our Prince's perspective during times of pain. Ask God to reveal to you who in your life can serve as a godly teammate. (Don't disregard parents—they have a special anointing from God to invest into your life.) Write down the person (or people) whom He lays on your heart.

My beloved is mine, and I am his. (Song of Solomon 2:16)

Life Meaning: When we are in Christ and Christ is in us, everything else pales in comparison to that amazing reality. We gladly lay all on the altar before Him, knowing that He holds our lives and our hearts in the palm of His hands.

6. Do you think of Christ's love for you as temporary or conditional? Read **Song of Solomon 2:4; Lamentations 3:22; Hosea 2:19;** and **Romans 8:38–39** and allow your perspective on Christ's love for you to be aligned with truth. Write down what He is speaking to your heart.

7. In what ways have you approached Christ with a "temporary relationship" mentality, even subconsciously? Are you ready to make a commitment to remain faithful to the One who will remain faithful to you forever? In your own words, express your eternal "vow" to offer your life in faithfulness to your heavenly Bridegroom.

OVERCOMING ROADBLOCKS

Can I experience a beautiful love story even if I have lost my purity?
Absolutely. When you have repented and turned from your sin, God washes you
clean, as white as snow. He does not punish you with a second-rate version of love
and romance. Eric and I are living testimonies of the fact that we serve a God of
new beginnings. Let your heart be encouraged by this excerpt from *When God
Writes Your Love Story:*

> The beauty of a God-written love story is not something reserved for the
> perfect and pious; it's for sinners like you and like me. That's what God's
> love is all about. We are so unworthy of His grace and forgiveness—and yet
> He offers it to us freely. If you have fallen in this area of your life and have
> asked yourself the question, "Is it too late for me?" read John 8:1–11 and
> take a close look at how Jesus responded to the woman caught in adultery.
> When we come to Him, bleeding and broken, filled with pain and regret,
> afraid to look into His eyes…He smiles tenderly. He lifts our chin with His
> nail-scarred hands. And He gently says, "I don't condemn you. Now go,
> and stop sinning."
>
> When we come face to face with this perfect love, it takes our breath
> away. We deserve to die for what we have done. We should be stoned by an
> angry mob. But not only does Jesus save our life with His own blood, He
> washed us completely clean. When He looks at us, He doesn't see our fail-
> ures and mistakes—He sees a new creation, a child of God.
>
> He tells us to "go and sin no more." He is speaking of repentance. This
> is the act of humbling ourselves, confessing our sin, and determining in our
> heart to turn and walk away from our sin from this day forward. Repentance
> literally means turning from our sin and walking in the other direction. With

His tender guiding hand in our lives, we can repent…and be made new. When we repent and accept His forgiveness, He can take the sin that our Enemy meant to use to destroy us, and use it for His glory. He can take a shattered heart and life and script a beautiful tale of His perfect love.[34]

Restoration

(BY BRIANNE, 25, WISCONSIN)

Before I came to Christ, I lost my purity. I gave away my heart, my body, and my innocence. I mingled with the world's destructive delicacies, I bought into the bondage-making lies of the culture and our Enemy, and I sought love, affection, and worth in all the wrong places. So if you are feeling like you are past the point of restoration, believe me, I know what you are going through.

But I also know without a doubt that restoration is possible through Jesus Christ. It is His life that has changed me. Do you know that the depths of His love and healing exceed whatever you have done? There is no place unreachable to Jesus. He extends His grace to you where you are in order to free you. "So if the Son sets you free, you will be free indeed" (John 8:36, NIV).

Be careful that you do not take this amazing gift of forgiveness lightly or use it as an excuse to live selfishly. Turn and walk toward the light instead of toward the darkness. Offer Him your whole existence from this day forward, and you will be amazed at how faithful your God will be.

If you have messed up in your past as I have, Jesus can purify you and restore you as a spotless, beautiful bride—His bride. Jesus calls you into a relationship with Himself, a covenant that is considered a spiritual marriage. He offers this to you because He loves you, cherishes you, and wants to set you free from your past—and maybe your present—to showcase His glory to the world around you. Jesus is calling you near to Himself so that He can give you the love and healing your heart needs.

I know it's not easy to comprehend or accept this truth. You may be saying, "You just don't understand my situation." But you are not alone in your struggles, in your darkness, or in the hurts of your past. Others have walked that path; I have walked that path, and Jesus knows it all.

Jesus and only Jesus can set you free to live the beautiful life He intended for you. He promises to restore you if you will trust Him and come. His arms are open wide, and He's waiting for you.

The Making of Poets

1. Do you know any guys like Chuck? Have you ever been tempted to settle for a "Chuck" simply because you didn't see anything better? How might God want to raise your standards in what you are waiting for in a guy?

2. Do you ever use nagging, criticism, or manipulation to try to change the guys in your life? What is the result when you do? How might God want to shift your tack from nagging to guy-nudging? Name some practical ways you can apply this in your interaction with guys, starting today.

3. Do you speak negatively of guys because you have been hurt or disgusted by men? How can you become a defender of Christ-built masculinity? What are some practical ways that you can be a Christ-like encourager, rather than a discourager, toward the men in your life?

Final Thoughts

IN EVERY GENERATION, there are a few young women who discover passionate, daily, unhindered intimacy with their true Prince, Jesus Christ…

Thanks be to God, who always leads us in triumphal procession in Christ and through us spreads everywhere the fragrance of the knowledge of him. (2 Corinthians 2:14, NIV)

QUESTIONS FOR DISCUSSION OR REFLECTION

1. What has been the overarching theme of this book for you? What has God been speaking to your heart the most on this journey?

2. After working through this study, do you think, act, or live differently? Have new habits been formed in any areas of your life? Describe the ways you have changed.

3. Which of the three historical examples of set-apart young women (Amy Carmichael, Esther Ahn Kim, or Betsy ten Boom) most challenged you? Why?

4. After going on this journey, who is Jesus Christ to you? In what ways have you grown to know Him more since you began this study?

5. As you go forward as one of the few in this generation who has chosen a set-apart life for your Prince, how can you keep the fire alive? Write down some practical ways to remember who you are in Him and what He has called you to.

"Trust Me, My child," He says. "Trust Me with a fuller abandon than you ever have before. Trust Me, as minute succeeds minute, every day of your life, for as long as you live. And if you become conscious of anything hindering our relationship, do not hurt Me by turning away from Me. Draw all the closer to Me, come, run to Me. Allow Me to hide you, to protect you, even from yourself. Tell Me your deepest cares, your every trouble. Trust Me to keep My hand upon you. I will never leave you. I will shape you, mold you, and perfect you. Do not fear, O child of My love, do not fear. I love you."

AMY CARMICHAEL[35]

Notes

1. Eric Ludy and Leslie Ludy, *When Dreams Come True* (Sisters, OR: Multnomah, 2004), 72.

2. Charles Spurgeon, "Return, Return, O Shulamite! Return, Return!" www.spurgeongems.org, vol. 28–30, sermon 1794.

3. Elisabeth Elliot, *Passion and Purity* (Tarrytown, NY: Revell, 1984), 131–32.

4. Quoted in Amy Carmichael, *Gold Cord* (London: Society for Promoting Christian Knowledge, 1947), 12.

5. Amy Carmichael, *God's Missionary* (Fort Washington, PA: Christian Literature Crusade, 1998), 24.

6. Henry Blackaby, *Experiencing God* (Nashville, TN: Lifeway, 1990), 19.

7. Oswald Chambers, *The Complete Works of Oswald Chambers*, comp. Biddy Chambers (Grand Rapids, MI: Discovery, 2000), 743.

8. Charles Spurgeon, "Evening Devotionals," www.blueletterbible.org, July 17.

9. Carmichael, *God's Missionary*, 39.

10. Charles E. Hummel, *Tyranny of the Urgent!* (Downers Grove, IL: InterVarsity, 1994), 5–6.

11. Elliot, *Passion and Purity*, 41.

12. Quoted in V. Raymond Edman, *They Found the Secret* (Grand Rapids, MI: Zondervan, 1984), 154–55.

13. Eric Ludy and Leslie Ludy, *When God Writes Your Love Story* (Sisters, OR: Multnomah, 2004), 141–42.

14. Elisabeth Dodds, *Marriage to a Difficult Man* (Philadelphia: Westminster, 1971), 17.

15. Wendy Shalit, *A Return to Modesty* (New York: Simon & Schuster, 1999), 85–86.

16. Unknown Author, "Learning Christ," www.catholic-kids.com/prayers.htm.

17. Elliot, *Passion and Purity*, 60–61.

18. Quoted in Carmichael, *God's Missionary,* 39.

19. Carmichael, *God's Missionary,* 39.

20. Chambers, *The Complete Works,* 832.

21. Ian Thomas, *The Indwelling of Christ* (Sisters, OR: Multnomah, 2006), 88.

22. A. W. Tozer, *The Divine Conquest* (Wheaton, IL: Tyndale, 1995), 7.

23. Eric Ludy and Leslie Ludy, *When God Writes Your Life Story* (Sisters, OR: Multnomah, 2004), 93–94.

24. Helen Keller, *The Story of My Life* (New York: Bantam Classics, 1990).

25. Quoted in Edman, *They Found the Secret,* 88.

26. Quoted in Carmichael, *Gold Cord,* 159–62.

27. Chambers, *The Complete Works,* 844.

28. Carmichael, *Gold Cord,* 40.

29. Ian Thomas, *The Mystery of Godliness* (Grand Rapids, MI: Zondervan, 1964), 162.

30. Amy Carmichael, *If* (Fort Washington, PA: Christian Literature Crusade, 1938), 60.

31. Chambers, *The Complete Works,* 711.

32. Tozer, *The Divine Conquest,* 53–54.

33. Eric Ludy and Leslie Ludy, *Teaching True Love to a Sex-at-13 Generation* (Nashville, TN: W Publishers, 2005), 69–73.

34. Ludy and Ludy, *When God Writes Your Love Story,* 226–29.

35. Carmichael, *If,* 93.

About the Author

LESLIE LUDY and her husband, Eric, are best-selling authors and speakers known for tackling some of the toughest relationship issues facing young people today. They have toured extensively, speaking to hundreds of thousands of teens, college students, parents, and leaders around the United States and abroad. Their passion is to motivate their generation to pursue a life completely transformed by Jesus Christ. Leslie and Eric have authored ten books including *When God Writes Your Love Story, When Dreams Come True, God's Gift to Women,* and *Teaching True Love to a Sex-at-13 Generation.* Leslie heads up Authentic Girl Ministries, a national fellowship for young women designed to encourage and equip set-apart femininity through conferences, discipleship groups, and resources. She and Eric live in Colorado with their toddler son, Hudson.

authentic*girl*
MINISTRIES
In every generation there are a few ...

Tools to equip you in your set-apart journey ...

Discipleship Training Conferences
With Eric and Leslie Ludy

- lay the foundation for historic Christianity in your own life
- explore the Bible in a whole new way
- be personally discipled by Eric and Leslie

Authentic Girl National Conferences
with Leslie Ludy

- experience a life-changing weekend
- fall in love with Christ like never before

Authentic Girl Fellowship Groups
- connect with other set-apart young women in your area

Authentic Girl Magazine
- cultivate Authentic Beauty in every aspect of your life

Visit www.authenticgirl.com
TO LEARN MORE!

Unabridged Audiobook

NOW AVAILABLE!

Authentic Beauty
- the unabridged audio book,
read by Leslie Ludy
Includes 30 minutes of candid discussion
with Leslie about Authentic Beauty!

Available on CD or for audio download at
www.authenticgirl.com

ALSO AVAILABLE:

When God Writes Your Love Story
- the unabridged audio book, read by Eric and Leslie Ludy

God's Gift to Women
- the unabridged audio book read by Eric Ludy

When God Writes Your Life Story
- the unabridged audio book, read by Eric and Leslie Ludy

When Dreams Come True
- the unabridged audio book, read by Eric and Leslie Ludy

OTHER BOOKS
BY ERIC AND LESLIE LUDY

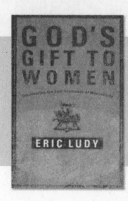

WHEN GOD WRITES YOUR LOVE STORY

Lay the foundation now—whether you've met your future spouse or not—for a lifelong romance that will stand the test of time. This book offers a whole new approach to building relationships...discover how beautiful your love story can be when the true Author of romance scripts every detail.

WHEN DREAMS COME TRUE

Be encouraged and inspired by Eric and Leslie's own love story—written in an engaging novel-style, about the decisions and mistakes they made in relationships before they met, how their friendship formed and grew, and the way God beautifully scripted the details of their romance. This story offers hope and vision for anyone in search of a love worth waiting for, and practical insight for those already in a relationship. It's a book you won't want to put down once you've started.

GOD'S GIFT TO WOMEN
- DISCOVERING THE LOST GREATNESS OF MASCULINITY

Wondering how to motivate the guys in your life toward Warrior Poet manhood? God's Gift to Women delivers an inspiring, candid and practical message about the state of modern manhood and paints a powerful picture of what masculinity is meant to be. It's a must-read for today's guys and today's girls. It's a perfect gift for guy friends, boyfriends and brothers!

WHEN GOD WRITES YOUR LIFE STORY

Whether you're currently tackling major life decisions or simply longing to live a life that really counts, When God Writes Your Life Story will infuse you with vision and purpose. This book introduces the amazing journey that awaits us when we step into God's endless frontier. It showcases the heroic potential of the true Christian life. The God of the Universe wants to write your life story. And when He does, you mustn't expect a mediocre tale!